AF412472

Naomi Leshem
RUNWAYS

Herausgegeben von / Edited by Michael Guggenheimer & Peter Röllin

Benteli

Naomi Leshem
RUNWAYS

Vom Verschwinden und Vergehen
Naomi Leshems Orte des Abschieds, Orte des Wandels

Lange war solide Architekturfotografie das Arbeitsgebiet von Naomi Leshem. Innenaufnahmen von Wohnbereichen und Geschäftsbauten, Bilder von neuen Bauten im Auftrag von Zeitschriften, Bauherren und Entwerfern. Heute erzählen die grossformatigen farbigen Bilder der in Tel Aviv lebenden Fotografin Geschichten vom Verschwinden und Vergehen.

Ein stille Wasserfläche, ein See im leichten Dunst der Morgendämmerung, in der Ferne ein Höhenzug und auf dem Wasser ein Boot, ein etwas heruntergekommenes Ausflugsschiff. Der See ein Abschiedsort. Hier hat ein Pilot mit seiner Kampfmaschine bei einem Wendemanöver die Höhe über Wasser angesichts der starken Blendung nicht richtig einschätzen können. Eine Flügelspitze des Militärflugzeugs hat die Seeoberfläche berührt, die Maschine mit ihrer Besatzung ist mit voller Wucht im See zerschellt, die beiden Männer, Pilot und Navigator, haben an dieser Stelle, die Naomi Leshem zwölf Jahre nach dem Unfall aufsucht, ihr Leben verloren. Es ist der See Genezareth, 210 Meter unter dem Meeresspiegel, von dessen Ufer aus sich die Fotografin genau hat zeigen lassen, wo die Maschine in die Tiefe gesunken ist.

Naomi Leshem ist Orten des Verschwindens und der Trennung nachgegangen. Eine Strasse in der Wüste, ein Asphaltband mit einer durchgezogenen weissen Sicherheitslinie und einem gelben Randstreifen, Palmen in der Ferne und brauner Sand zu beiden Seiten der Strassenpiste, die Stelle, wo eine junge Frau bei einem Motorradunfall ihr Leben gelassen hat. Mit der Mutter der Toten hat sie zwei Tage verbracht, hat sich das Leben und die Umstände des tödlichen Unfalls erzählen lassen, um dann den letzten Ort eines Lebens zu fotografieren. Zwölf Stunden Autofahrt nimmt ein Elternpaar mehrmals im Jahr auf sich, um jene Stelle in der Negevwüste aufzusuchen, an der ihr Sohn mit einem Flugzeug abgestürzt ist, als ein Vogel in das Triebwerk der Maschine geriet und der Pilot die Beherrschung über den Flugkörper verlor. Beim Zerschellen auf dem Wüstenboden hat die Maschine einen Krater gebildet, an dessen Rand die Eltern jeweils stehen bleiben. Im Sand glitzern manche Stellen im gleissenden Sonnenlicht, es sind die letzten sichtbaren Überreste jener Flugtragödie, kleine Metallsplitter, die an den Unfalltod erinnern. Ein schöner Ort, eine stille Landschaft, eine Stelle, an der die Eltern ihren Sohn innerlich suchen, an ihn denken, den Abschied immer wieder vollziehen.

Naomi Leshem hat den Ort festgehalten, nachdem sie mit den beiden gesprochen hat. Anders als ein Journalist oder als eine Schriftstellerin hält die Fotografin die Orte fest. Es sind nicht Worte, es sind keine geschriebenen Erzählungen, es sind Bilder, deren Bedeutung sich aus der Bildgeschichte erschliesst. Orte des Abschieds, deren Geschichte den Hinterbliebenen, den Trauernden vertraut ist. Ein altes Schwimmbad an der Strandpromenade von Tel Aviv, ein nicht mehr benutztes Meerwasserbecken, dessen Wände in rissig blauer Farbe leuchten, im Hintergrund weisse Segelmasten, die in die Höhe zeigen, davor Sonnenschirme und eine Wasserrutsche, die ebenfalls nicht mehr gebraucht werden. Hierher kommt ein Sohn in Begleitung der Fotografin, um jenen Ort aufzusuchen, an dem sein Vater ertrank. Oder ein Feld mit einem Haus im Hintergrund. Hier wurde ein Mann ermordet, ein Polizist, der die Schreie eines Menschen hörte, dem Angegriffenen zur Hilfe eilte, um dabei selber den Tod zu finden.

Ein Mal jeden Monat begibt sich Naomi Leshem zwischen dem 17. und 19. des Monats am Mittag an den Rand der Ortschaft Petach Tikva östlich von Tel Aviv, um dort jeweils vom Balkon einer Wohnung im 17. Stockwerk eines Wohnhauses ein Landschaftsbild einzufangen. Jeden Monat entsteht ein Bild. Die Bilder einer Serie tragen als Titel bloss Datumsangaben. Naomi Leshem richtet ihre Hasselblad gegen Osten in Richtung von Ariel, um die Landschaft zu fotografieren. In der Ferne sind die weissen Häuser der Stadt Ariel in den besetzten Gebieten der West Bank knapp zu erkennen. Wer sich die Bilderfolge anschaut, sieht, dass der grosse Friedhof in unmittelbarer Nachbarschaft der Wohnsiedlung von Petach Tikva kontinuierlich wächst, wie neue Grabreihen innert eines Monats hinzugekommen sind. Zu sehen ist auch, wie der Bau einer Tiefgarage und neuer Wohnhäuser voranschreitet. Während sich im Herbst die Spuren von Lastwagen auf den dürren Wiesen vor dem Friedhof noch deutlich in die Erde eingraben, verschwinden die Spuren gegen Frühling mit jeder Aufnahme, da die Wiesen grüner werden. Besucher des Friedhofs sind auf den Bildern zu erkennen, vorbeifahrende Autos auf einer

Fernstrasse, am Horizont die Hügel Samarias. Es sind Zeichen der Veränderung einer Landschaft. Menschen werden beerdigt, andere nehmen in der Nähe
des Friedhofs ihren Wohnsitz. Jede Aufnahme zeigt den exakt gleichen Aus-
schnitt der Landschaft. Und doch unterscheiden sich die Aufnahmen stark
voneinander. Mal sind es dunkle Winterwolken, die einen Regenguss ankün-
den, ein anderes Mal ist es der Dunst des Sommers und der unerträglich
heisse Chamsinwind weht über die ausgetrocknete, dürre Ebene. Naomi Leshem
hat die Serie, die sie nach der Besitzerin der Wohnung „Lizette" nennt,
eher zufällig angefangen. Es war das Erstaunen über die Weite der Landschaft und über die Nähe von Friedhof und Wohnsiedlung, die sie reizte.
Mittlerweile macht Lizette mit, beobachtet zwischen den Besuchen der Fotografin die Landschaft sehr genau, berichtet ihr jeweils, was sich in der
Zwischenzeit vor dem Balkon und so weit das Auge reicht, verändert hat.

Naomi Leshem arbeitet mit einer analogen Kamera und Stativ. Mitten
auf den Abflug- und Landepisten israelischer Miltärflughäfen hat sie sich po-
stiert, um dort, wo Düsenjäger und Bomber unter mächtigem Lärm starten und
landen eine Bilderfolge zu machen. Auf halber Bildhöhe berühren sich auf
diesen Fotografien Himmel und Erde. Und immer ist auf der Piste eine junge Frau zu sehen — manchmal sind es auch zwei Frauen —, die sich auf dem
Rollfeld in Richtung des Horizonts wegbewegt oder wegrennt. Es sind junge
Frauen, die die in Israel obligatorische Militärdienstzeit vor sich haben, friedliche Frauen auf den Pisten der todbringenden Militärmaschinen.
Wieder treffen sich hier Leben und Tod, Sein und Verschwinden, eine Motiv-
kombination, die Naomi Leshems Bildersprache prägt. Die harten Bremsspuren
auf den Pisten deuten jene Wucht an, mit denen die Flugzeuge zum Anhalten
gebracht werden. Die Landschaften zu beiden Seiten der Piste deuten die
verschiedenen Vegetationsregionen des Landes an: Wüstensand, Meeresdünen,
industrielle Bauten am Horizont, grüne Hügel. Ebenso wie die Bilder, die
sie von Lizettes Balkon aus festhält, sind auch diese Fotografien alle zur
Mittagszeit entstanden, in jener Stunde, da die Pistenbeläge sengend hei-
ss sind. Die Tageszeit ist mit Absicht gewählt, denn die Schatten der jun-
gen Frauen sollen auf den Fotografien möglichst klein sein.

Wenn Naomi Leshem ihre quadratischen farbigen Bilderserien zeigt, dann führt sie noch eine weitere Serie von Fotografien in den Zyklus ein. Es sind Bilder, die von Braun-, Grün- und Gelbtönen beherrscht sind, Fotografien, auf denen Metallteile in Silbergrau glänzen, manchmal sind Objekte in Rot und Orange zu erkennen: Unterwasserbilder, die von einem ferngesteuerten Roboter in der Tiefe des See Genezareth auf der Höhe der Ortschaft Ein Gev am Fuss der Golanhöhen aufgenommen wurden, Bilder vom Wrack jenes Düsenjägers, dessen Pilot und Navigator am Mittag des 5. Mai 1991 in den Fluten des Sees umgekommen sind. Naomi Leshem hat Jahre nachdem sie ihre Bilder von der Absturzstelle gemacht hat, von den Untersuchungsbehörden die Videoaufnahmen von der Suche nach der Blackbox und nach anderen Teilen des Wracks erhalten. Ausschnitte davon hat sie in Form von Stills zu einer Bilderfolge zusammengestellt. Auf dem Boden des Sees gibt es Zeichen von Bewegung, Sand wirbelt auf, wie hinter Nebelschleiern zeigen sich Teile des Flugzeugs, dessen Eingeweide auf dem Seegrund verstreut liegen, technische Aufschriften, Objekte, deren Funktion sich dem unkundigen Betrachter nicht erschliessen, weshalb sie auch aus dem Innern eines Körpers stammen könnten. Die Bilder der Zerstörung sind von ambivalenter Schönheit.

Orte bleiben, während die Menschen, die sie bevölkern, wieder verschwinden: Bilder einer anderen, in unserer Publikation nicht enthaltenen Serie von Naomi Leshem, halten Räume fest, an denen sich Menschen regelmässig einfinden, auf andere stossen, den Ort wieder verlassen, um sich ein anderes Mal, Wochen oder Monate später wieder hier einzufinden. Ein Wohnzimmer etwa, in dem sich Grosseltern mit ihren erwachsenen Kindern und den Enkelkindern treffen. Stunden später sind sie wieder weg, sind sie nur noch schemenhaft auf dem Bild zu erkennen. Die Spielsachen der Kinder sind bereits teilweise aufgeräumt, das Wohnzimmer, in dem sich siebzehn Personen aus drei Generationen aufgehalten haben, ist wieder still, das laute Durcheinander der Stimmen ist verstummt. Die Menschen, die sich hier immer wieder sehen, werden bei jedem Treffen älter, sie verändern sich, tragen von Mal zu Mal andere Kleider, kommen mit ihren stets neuen Geschichten zusammen, während der Ort unverändert bleibt. Ein Hotelzimmer, ein Bett morgens,

Spuren einer Übernachtung, die Bewegung der Leintücher ist noch zu erkennen. Gäste kommen und verlassen den Ort, der stets der gleiche bleibt. Oder ein Fotostudio, in dem sich regelmässig Frauen und Männer zu Aufnahmen einfinden, Personenbilder werden hier aufgenommen, Porträts und Modeaufnahmen. Immer wieder ähnliche Situationen. Der Raum bleibt stets derselbe, die Positionen der Porträtierten vor der Leinwand ähneln sich. Veränderung und Wandel sind hier das Thema, das die Fotografin fasziniert. Ein Unterrichtsraum, Studenten, die zu einer Unterrichtsstunde zusammengekommen sind, wechselnde Benutzer desselben Raums. Der Raum nimmt sie auf, es ist der stets selbe Ort, den Tag für Tag andere aufsuchen. Oder ein Friedhof, Gräber, um die sich eine Gruppe von Menschen jedes Jahr zur Gedenkfeier trifft. Eine Stunde lang ein belebter Ort, der Trauerredner am Mikrofon ist zu sehen, die Trauergäste nur noch undeutlich, denn sie schicken sich bereits an wegzugehen. Die mitgebrachten Blumenkränze werden verblühen und dann entsorgt. Der Friedhof als Treffpunkt, ein Ort des Gedenkens, an dem sich ein Jahr später dieselbe Gruppe treffen wird.

On Disappearance and Death: Naomi Leshem's Sites of Farewell, Sites of Change

For a long time, solid architectural photography was Naomi Leshem's field: interiors of living spaces and industrial buildings, images of new buildings commissioned by journals, architects, and designers. Today, this Tel Aviv photographer's large-format color photographs tell tales of disappearance and death.

The peaceful surface of a lake in a slightly hazy dawn, with a mountain range in the distance and a somewhat rundown pleasure boat on the water. The lake as a site of farewell: here, while a jet-fighter pilot was performing a turning maneuver, extreme glare made it impossible for him to correctly estimate how far he was above the water. One of the plane's wingtips touched the surface of the lake; the plane and its crew crashed into the water at top speed. Two men, the pilot and the navigator, lost their lives at this site Leshem first visited twelve years later. It is the Sea of Galilee, 210 meters below sea level; from the shore, the photographer asked to be shown the precise spot where the plane had sunk into the depths.

Leshem sought out such sites of disappearance and parting. A road in the desert, an asphalt strip with a continuous white line in the middle and a yellow line along the side, with palms in the distance and brown sand on both sides of the road — here, a young woman died in a motorcycle accident. Leshem spent two days with the dead woman's mother, listening to her life story and learning the circumstances of the fatal accident; then, she photographed this final site in a life. Several times a year, two parents undertake a twelve-hour trip by car to visit the place in the Negev Desert where their son's airplane crashed when a bird got in the engine and the pilot lost control of the plane. The parents always stand at the edge of the crater formed where the plane hit the ground. In the sand, a few spots glitter in the glistening sunlight; they are the last visible remains of an air tragedy, little fragments of metal commemorating an accidental death. A beautiful place, a peaceful landscape, a site where the parents look for their son in their thoughts and memories and work through their farewell again and again.

Leshem took her photograph of this site after speaking with the parents. She does not work with her sites in the same way a journalist or a writer would. These are not words, not written stories; these are images whose meanings emerge from their backgrounds. Sites of farewell whose stories are familiar to the mourners. An old saltwater swimming pool by the beach promenade in Tel Aviv, now abandoned, its walls shining in cracked blue, with white masts pointing into the air in the background and sunshades now as unused as the water slide. Here, with the photographer, a son came to visit the place where his father drowned. Or a field with a house in the background. Here, a policeman, hearing someone screaming, ran to help and ended up being killed himself.

Between the 17th and the 19th of every month, Leshem goes at noon to the edge of the city of Petach Tikva, east of Tel Aviv, and takes a photograph of the landscape visible from a balcony on the 17th story of an apartment building. That is, there is a new photograph in this series every month, its title merely the date when it was taken. Leshem points her Hasselblad east to photograph the landscape; in the distance, the white houses of the city of Ariel in the occupied areas of the West Bank are just visible. The sequence of images reveals that the large cemetery immediately adjacent to this Petach Tikva housing development is continually growing, with new rows of graves added every month. It also marks the progress of the construction of an underground parking garage and of new apartment buildings. In the fall, the wheel marks that trucks dug into the barren fields in front of the cemetery are still clearly visible, but as spring comes and the fields grow greener, the tracks vanish with every photograph. Visitors to the cemetery are visible in the photographs, as are passing cars on a highway and the hills of Samaria on the horizon. These are signs of how a landscape changes. People are buried; others come to live near the cemetery. Each photograph frames the landscape in the exact same way. And yet each is significantly different from the others. Sometimes, dark winter clouds threaten a shower; sometimes, there is a summer haze, and the unbearably hot Khamsin wind blows across the dried, barren plains. Leshem started this series, which she calls "Lizette" (the name of the apartment's owner), more or less by chance. It was her astonishment at the dimensions of the landscape, as well as the proximity of the cemetery and the housing development, that attracted her. By now, Lizette participates in the project by observing the landscape very carefully between the photographer's visits and telling her what has changed since she was last there, both right in front of the balcony and as far as the eye can see.

Leshem works with an analog camera and a tripod. In the middle of the departure and arrival runways at Israel's military airports, she established a position to take a series of photographs amidst the horrendous din where jets and bombers start and land. Halfway up the image in each of these photographs, the sky and the earth meet. And a young woman (sometimes two) is always visible on the runway, walking or running away across the airfield toward the horizon. These young women have their obligatory military service ahead of them, these peaceful women on the runways of death-bringing military planes. Again, life and death meet here, being and disappearance, a combination of motifs that characterizes Leshem's pictorial language. The rough skid marks on the runways recall the violence with which the airplanes brake. The landscapes on both sides of the runway recall the country's various natural regions: desert sand, seaside dunes, industrial buildings on the horizon, green hills. Just like the photographs Leshem takes from Lizette's balcony, these photographs were also all taken at midday, when the runway surfaces are scorchingly hot. The time of day was intentional, for the shadows of the young women in the photographs are supposed to be as small as possible.

When Leshem exhibits her series of square-format color images, she introduces a second series of photographs into the cycle. These photographs are dominated by shades of brown, green, and yellow in which silver-gray metal parts shine. Sometimes, red and orange objects can be seen in these underwater images taken by a remote-controlled robot in the depths of the Sea of Galilee near the village Ein Gev at the foot of the Golan Heights. They are images of the wreck of that jet whose pilot and navigator died at noon on May 5, 1991, in these waters. Years after she had taken the photographs of the site of the accident, the investigating authorities gave Leshem the videos of the search for the black box and other parts of the wreck. She put stills from these videos together to form a series. At the bottom of the lake, there are signs of movement; sand churns up; parts of the plane can be seen as if behind veils of fog. Its inner workings lie scattered on the bottom of the lake: technical labels, and objects whose function cannot be determined by any observer who is not an expert, so that they seem as if they could also have come from inside a body. These images of destruction have an ambivalent beauty.

Places endure, while the people who inhabit them continually disappear: photographs in another series by Leshem (one not included here) were taken in places where people regularly gather, meet other people, and leave once more, only to gather there again weeks or months later. A living room, for example, where grandparents are visited by their adult children and grandchildren. Hours later, they have gone away again and have left only dim images in the photographs behind. The children's toys have been cleaned up, but not completely; the living room where seventeen people from three generations gathered is still again; the loud confusion of voices has fallen silent. The people who keep seeing each other here get older at every meeting; they change, wear different clothes every time, and meet again with their ever changing faces, but the place remains the same. A hotel room, a bed in the morning, the marks of an overnight stay, the movement of the sheets still visible. Guests come and go in this place that always remains the same. Or a photographer's studio where men and women regularly come for photographs, where pictures of people are taken, portraits and fashion photos. Similar situations over and over again. The space remains the same; the positions of the people whose portraits are being taken in front of the canvas are similar. Change and transformation are the themes that fascinate the photographer here. A classroom, students attending a lesson — the always changing users of the same room. The room absorbs them, always the same place, visited by different people day after day. Or

a cemetery, graves where a group of people meets every year for a memori-
al service. For one hour, a lively place, the eulogist at the microphone,
the mourners only just visible, already leaving. The wreaths they brought
along will fade and then be thrown away. The cemetery as a meeting point,
a site of memory, where, a year later, the same group will meet again.

Way to beyond

01   untitled for m #1

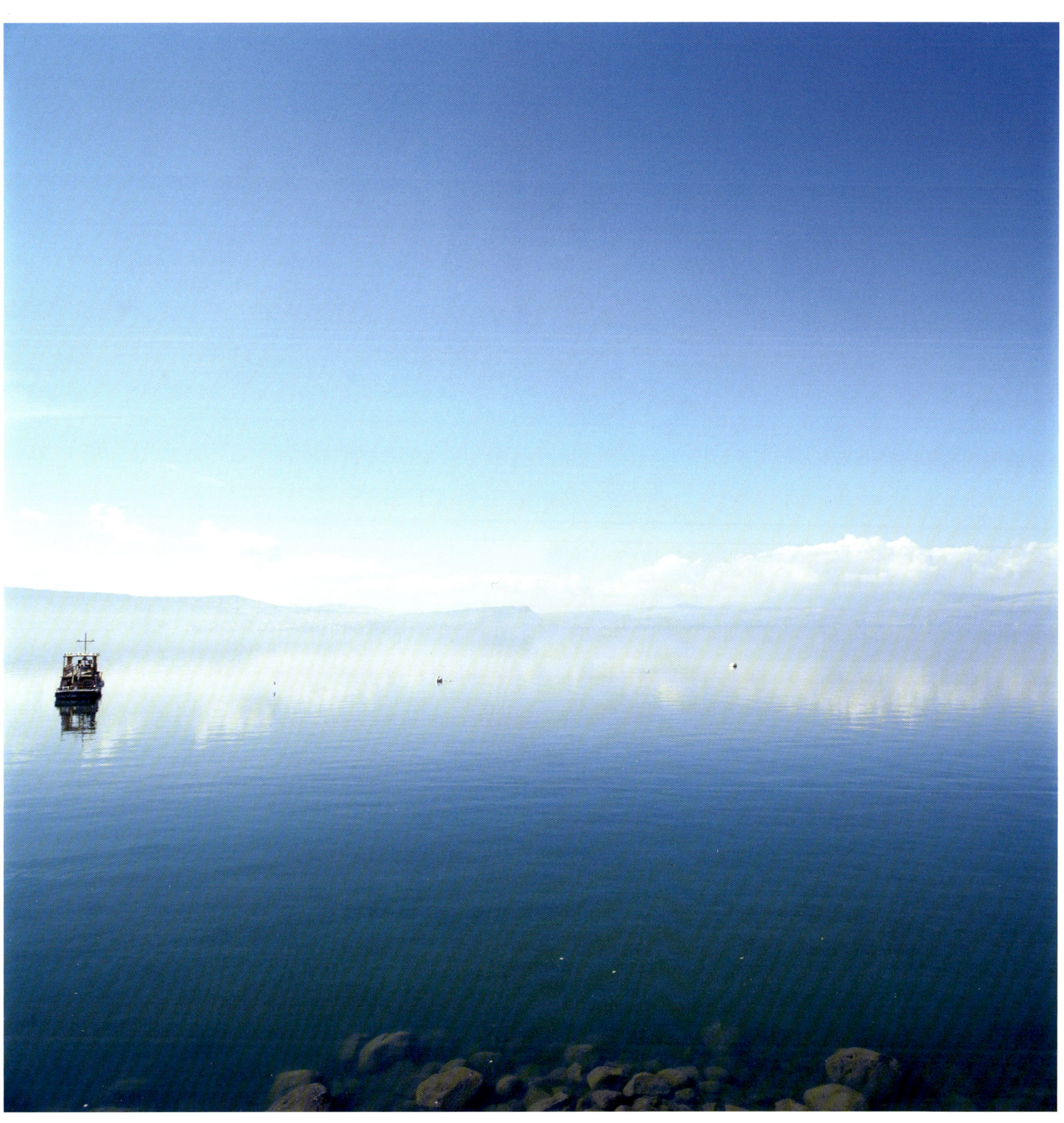

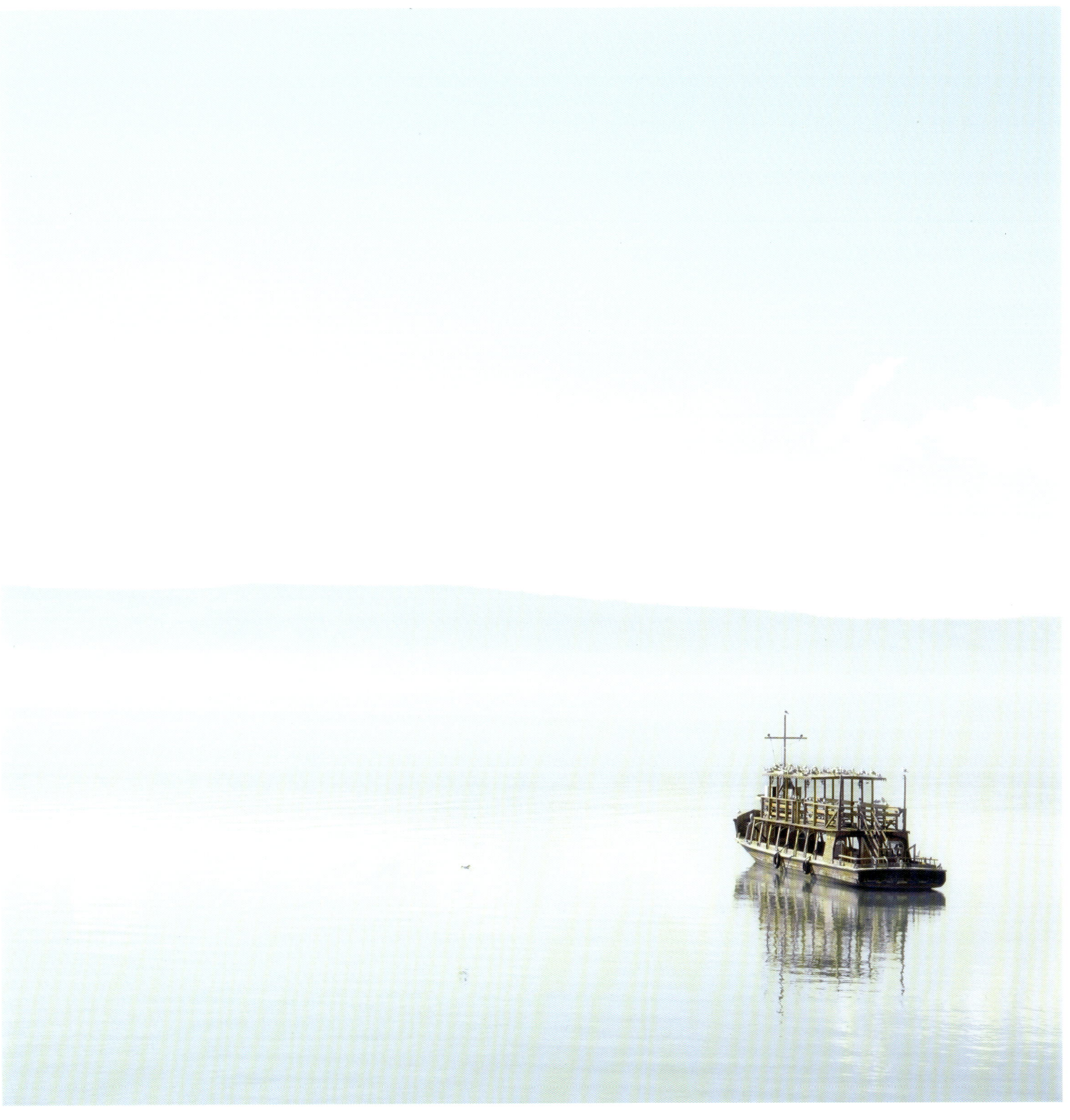

03   untitled #7

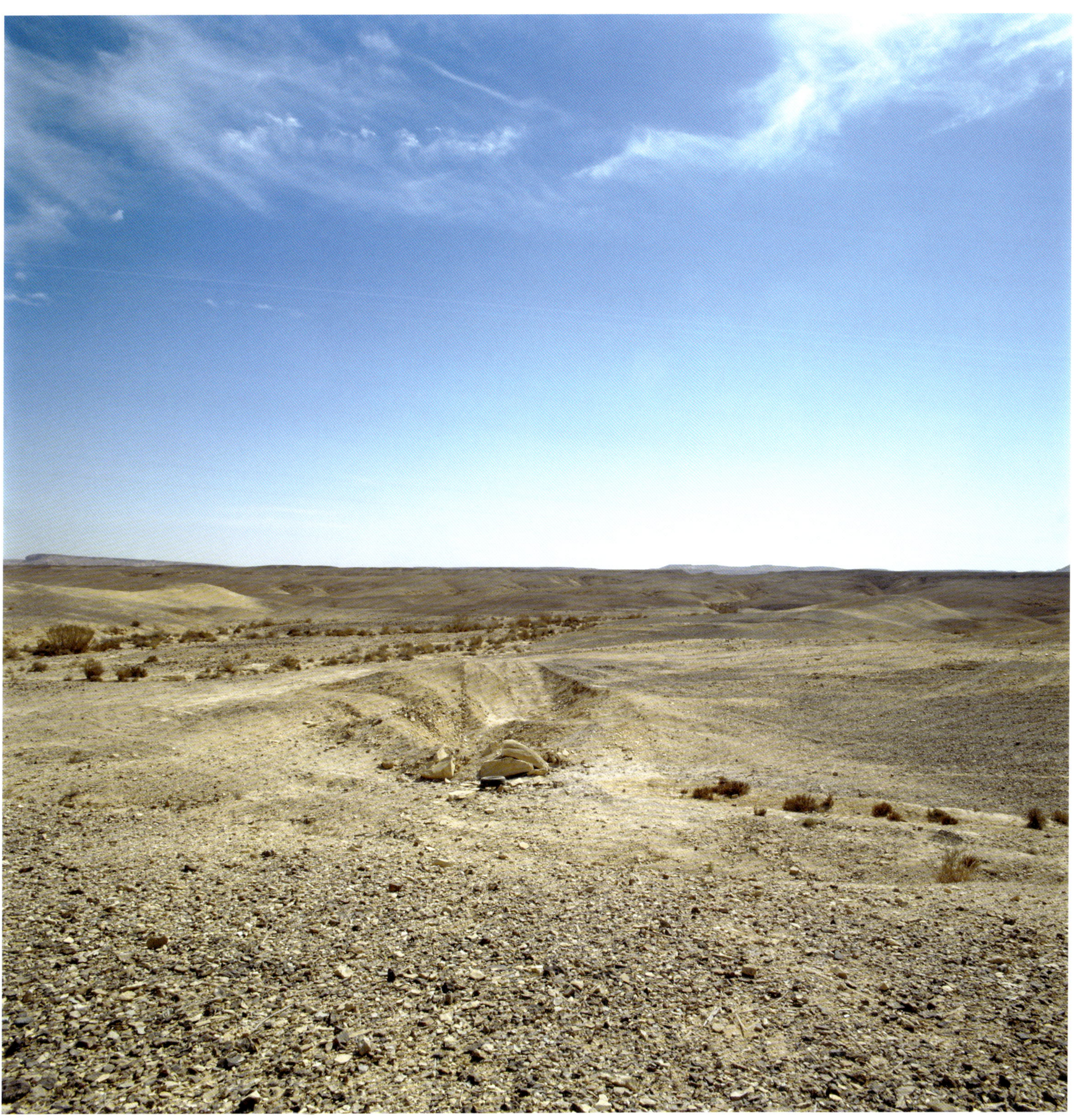

05   untitled #8

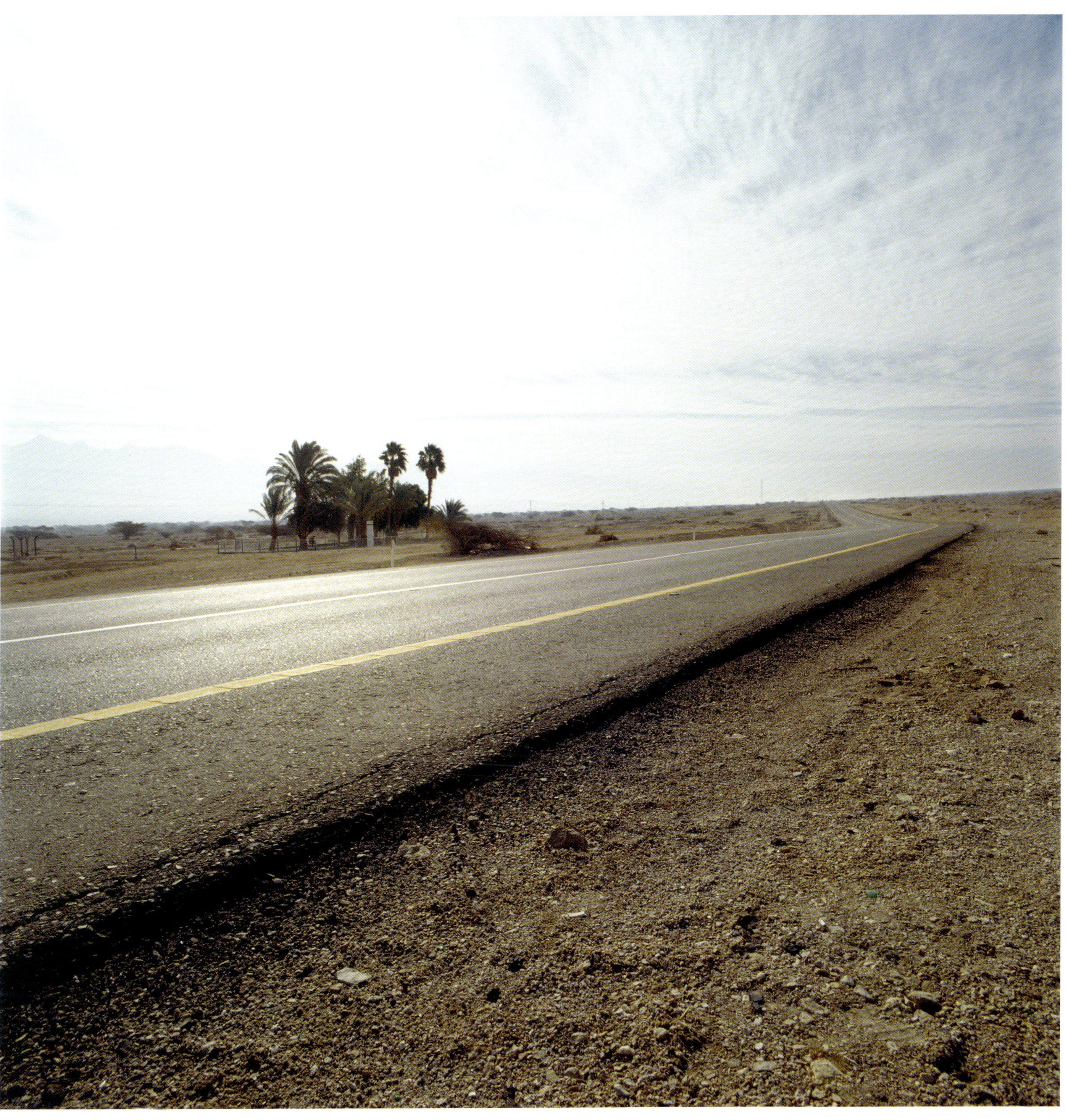

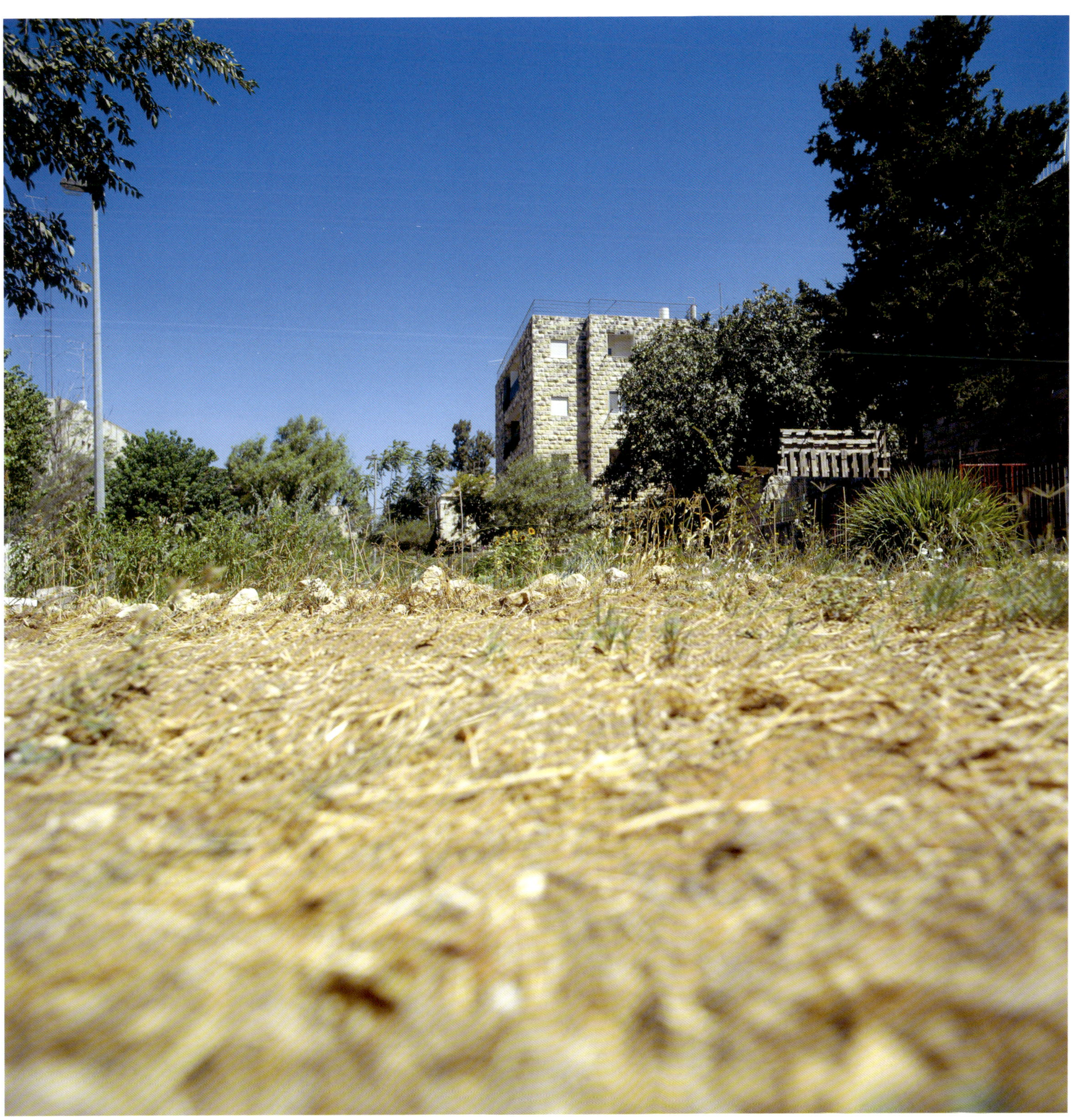

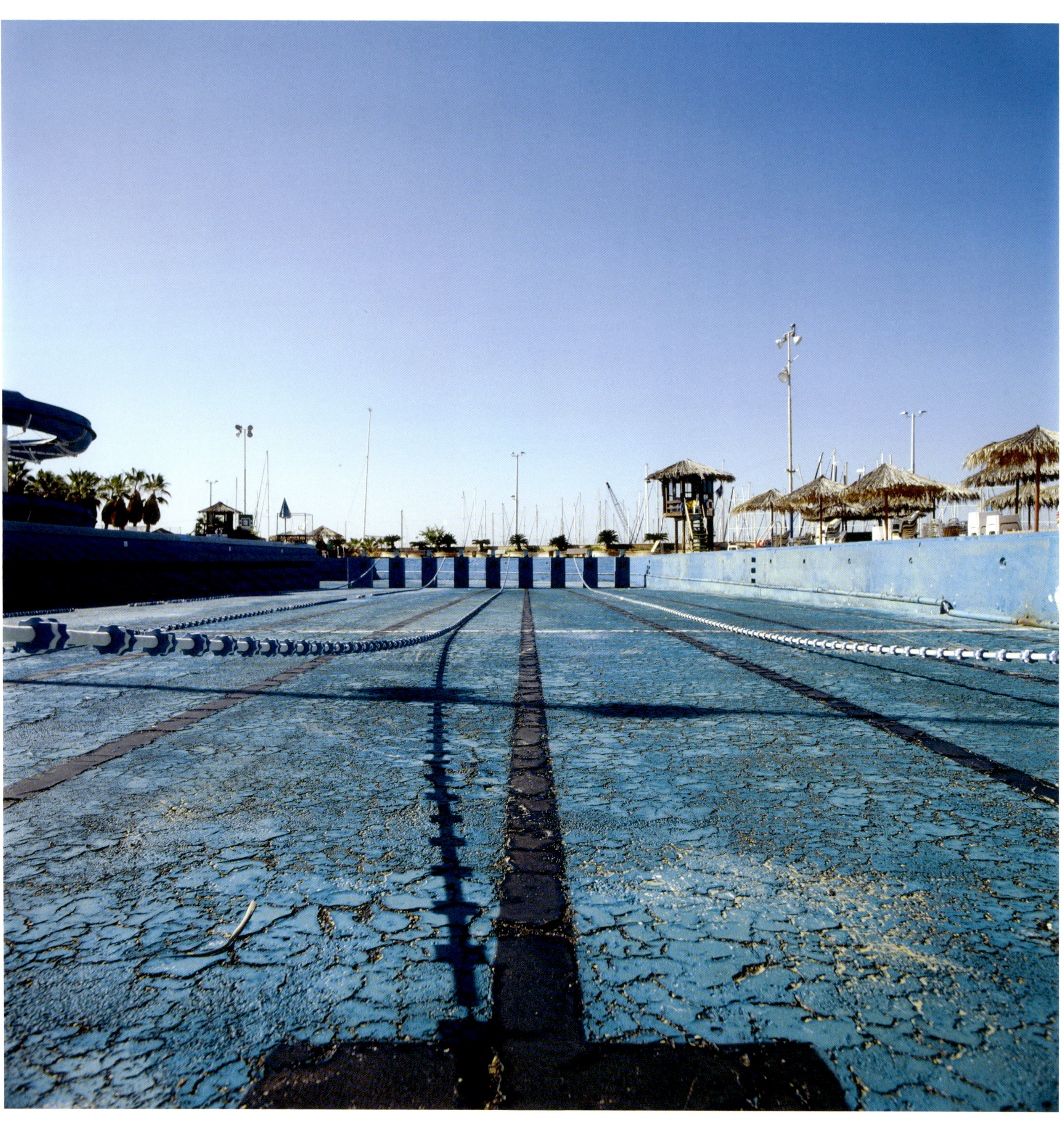

07   untitled #12

01 – 07   **Way to beyond**

2003   Orte des Verschwindens und des
01 / 02 / 06   Abschieds. In den Tiefen des Sees
                                 Genezareth, dort wo ein Boot
2004   ankert, liegt ein Flugzeugwrack.
03 / 04 / 05   Ein Krater im Wüstensand markiert
                                 die Stelle, an der ein Pilot mit
2006   einer anderen Maschine zerschellt
07   ist. Eine Motorradfahrerin ist
                                 auf der Schnellstrasse in den
                                 Süden tödlich verunglückt. Hinter
je 120 cm × 120 cm   einem Wohnhaus ist ein Polizist
c-Prints   erstochen worden, als er einem
auf 5 Exemplare begrenzte   Angegriffenen zur Hilfe eilte.
Edition + einem E.A.   Im Schwimmbad ist ein Mann ent-
                                 kräftet ertrunken.

each 47.24 in × 47.24 in
c-Print   Sites of disappearance and fare-
edition of 5 + 1 a.p.   well. In the depths of the Sea of
                                 Galilee, right where a boat is
                                 anchored, lies the wreckage of an
                                 airplane. A crater in the desert
                                 sand marks where a pilot crashed
                                 another airplane. A woman on a
                                 motorcycle had a fatal accident
                                 on a highway to the south. Behind
                                 an apartment building, a police-
                                 man was stabbed to death when
                                 he ran to help someone who was
                                 being attacked. In a swimming
                                 pool, an exhausted man drowned.

Phantom

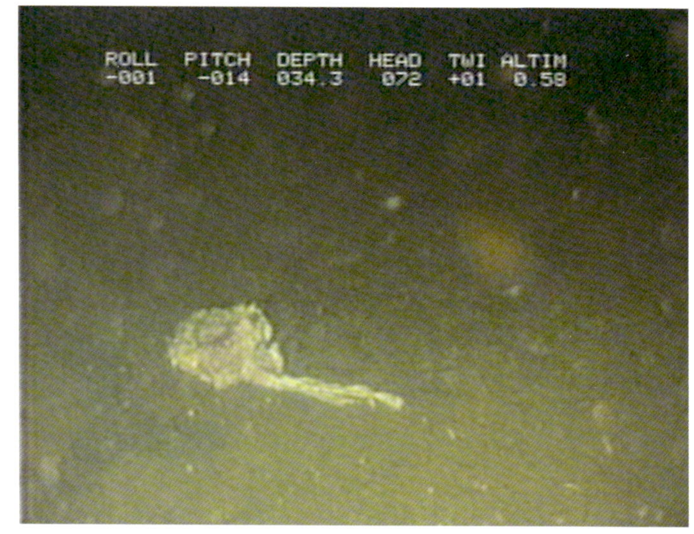
ROLL PITCH DEPTH HEAD TWI ALTIM
-001   -014   034.3   072   +01 0.58

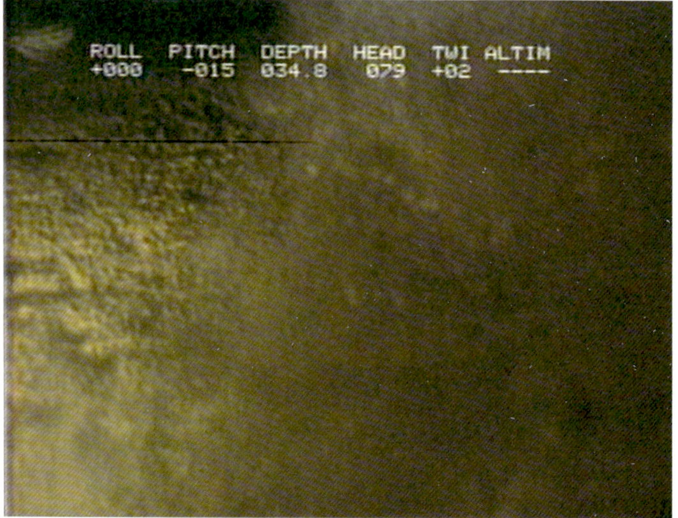
ROLL PITCH DEPTH HEAD TWI ALTIM
+000   -015   034.8   079   +02 ----

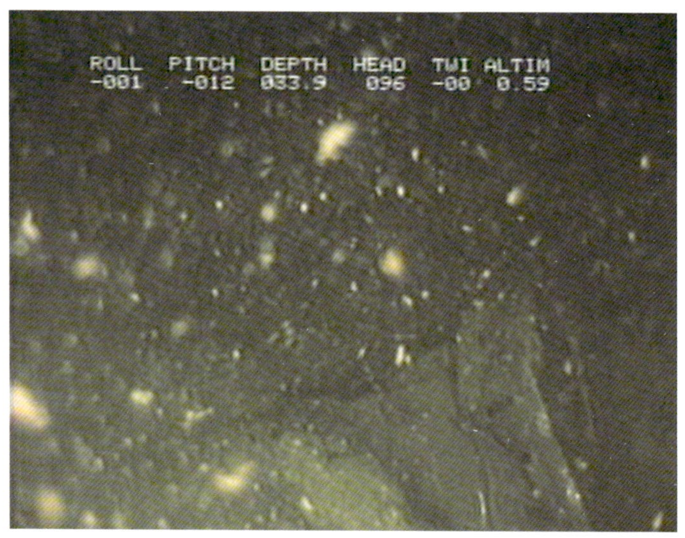
ROLL PITCH DEPTH HEAD TWI ALTIM
-001   -012   033.9   096   -00 0.59

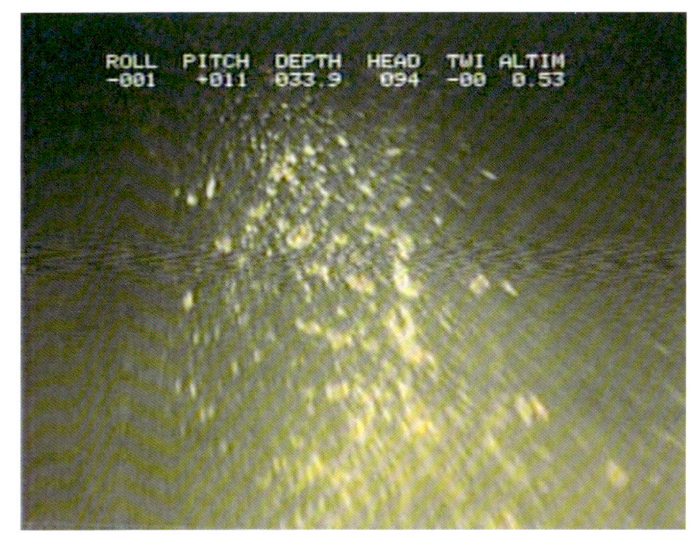

ROLL PITCH DEPTH HEAD TWI ALTIM
-001 +011   033.9   094 -00 0.53

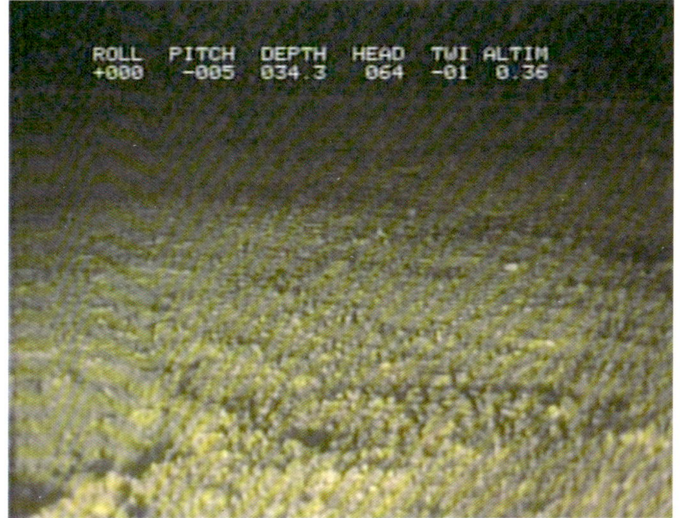

ROLL PITCH DEPTH HEAD TWI ALTIM
+000 -005   034.3   064 -01 0.36

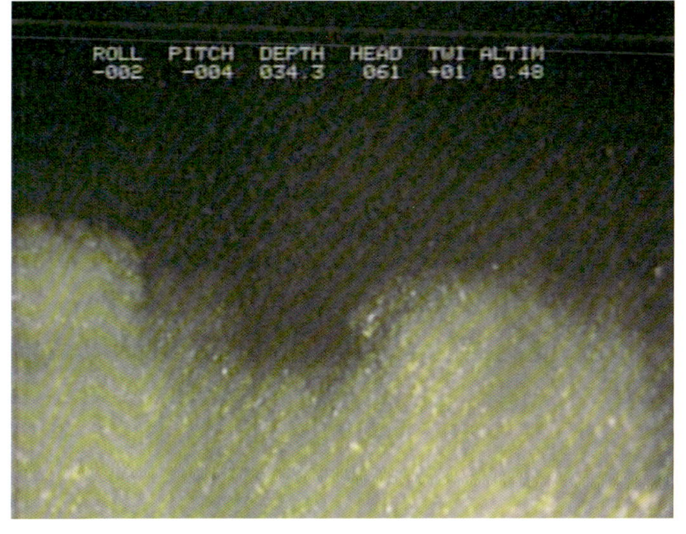

ROLL PITCH DEPTH HEAD TWI ALTIM
-002 -004   034.3   061 +01 0.48

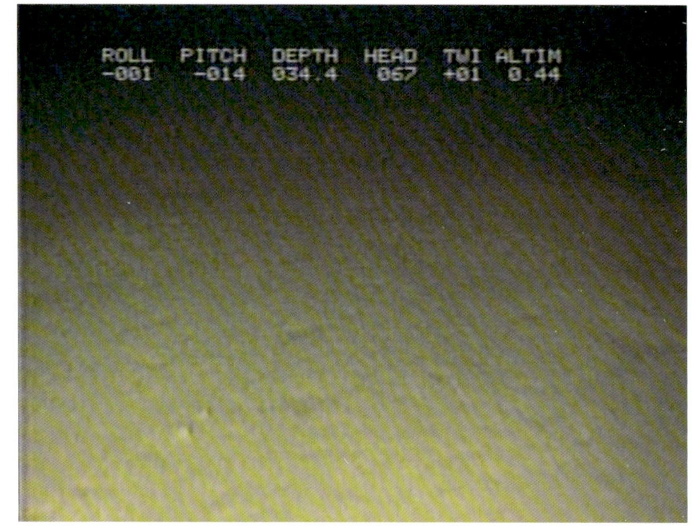
ROLL PITCH DEPTH HEAD TWI ALTIM
-001 -014   034.4 067   +01 0.44

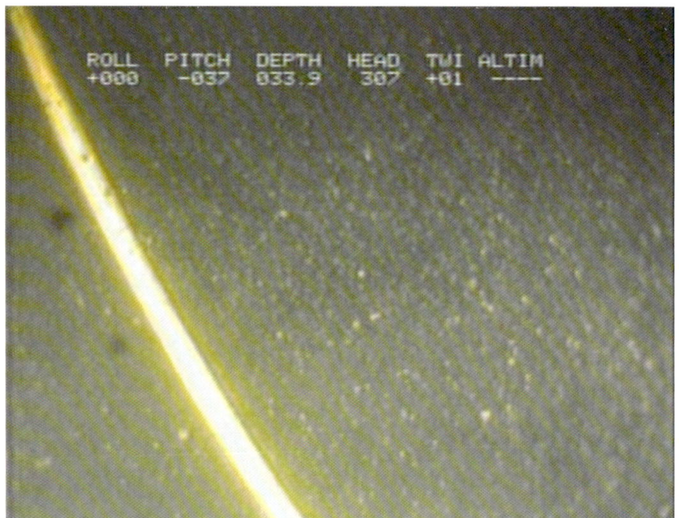
ROLL PITCH DEPTH HEAD TWI ALTIM
+000 -037   033.9 307   +01 ----

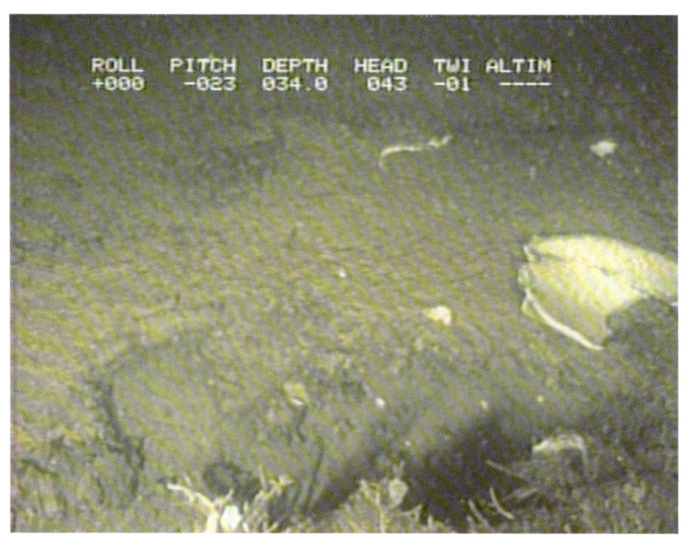
ROLL PITCH DEPTH HEAD TWI ALTIM
+000 -023   034.0 043   -01 ----

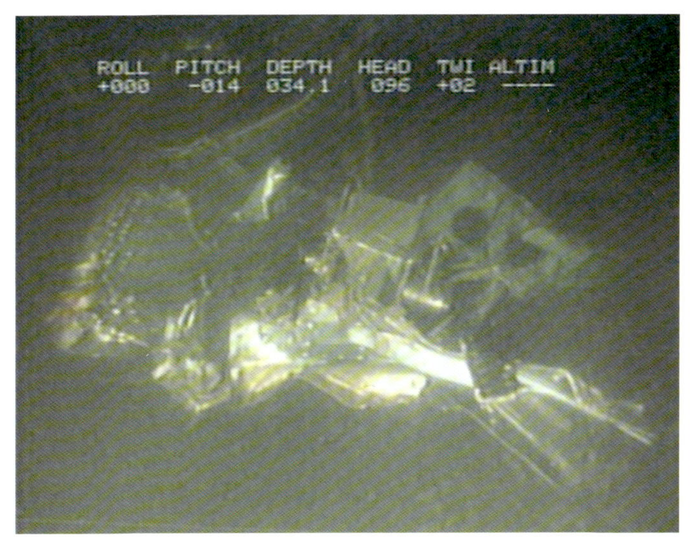

ROLL PITCH DEPTH HEAD TWI ALTIM
+000 -014   034.1 096   +02 ----

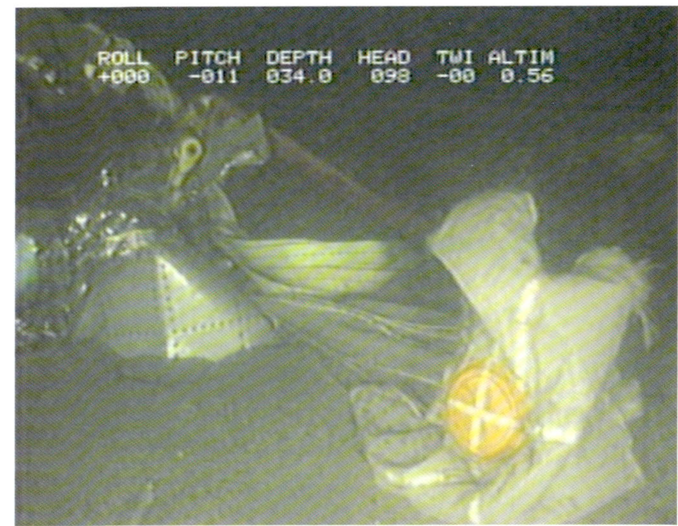

ROLL PITCH DEPTH HEAD TWI ALTIM
+000 -011   034.0 098   -00 0.56

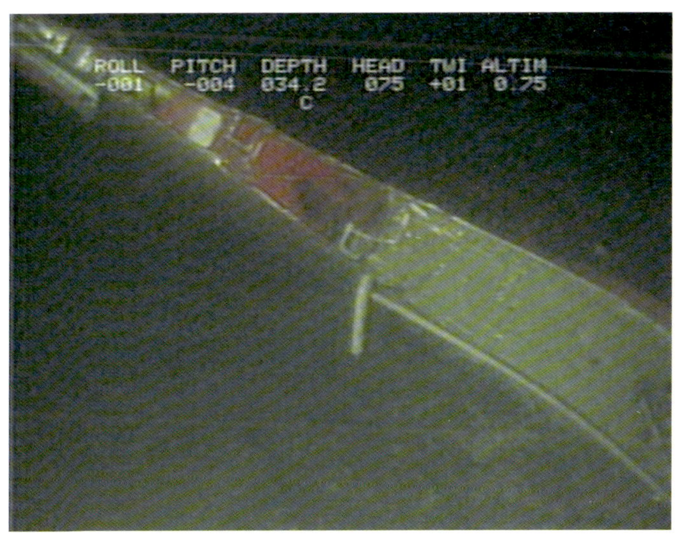

ROLL PITCH DEPTH HEAD TWI ALTIM
-001 -004   034.2 075   +01 0.75
C

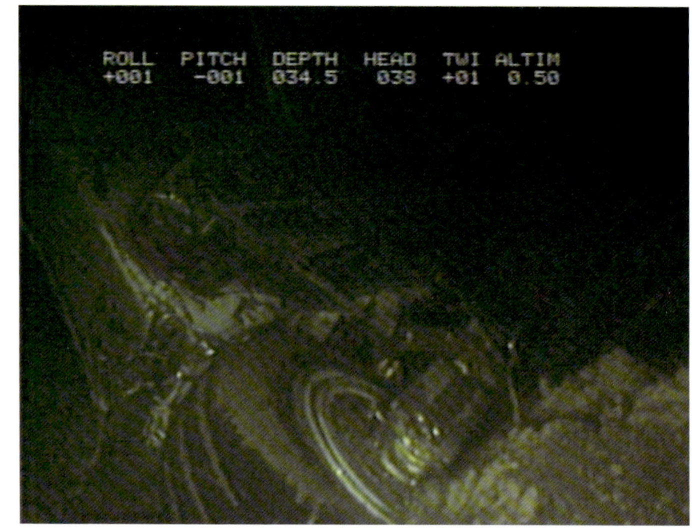
ROLL PITCH DEPTH HEAD TWI ALTIM
+001 -001 034.5 038 +01 0.50

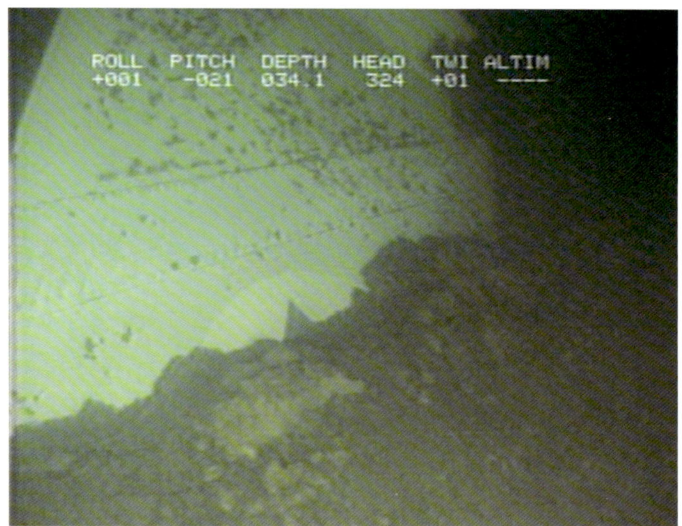
ROLL PITCH DEPTH HEAD TWI ALTIM
+001 -021 034.1 324 +01 ----

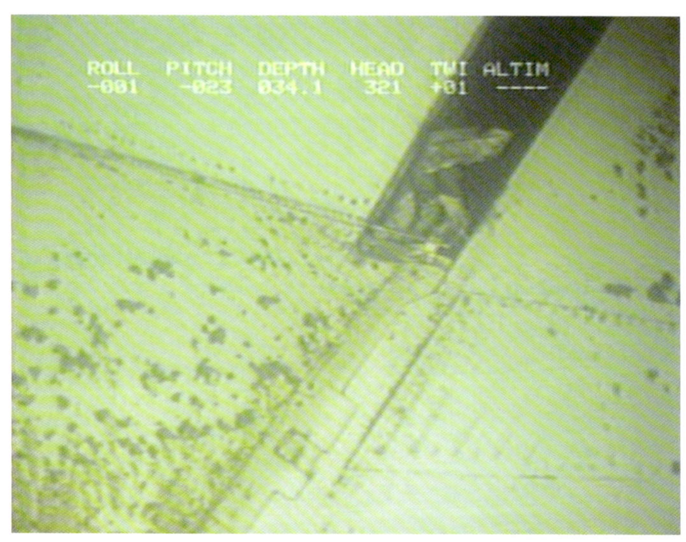
ROLL PITCH DEPTH HEAD TWI ALTIM
-001 -023 034.1 321 +01 ----

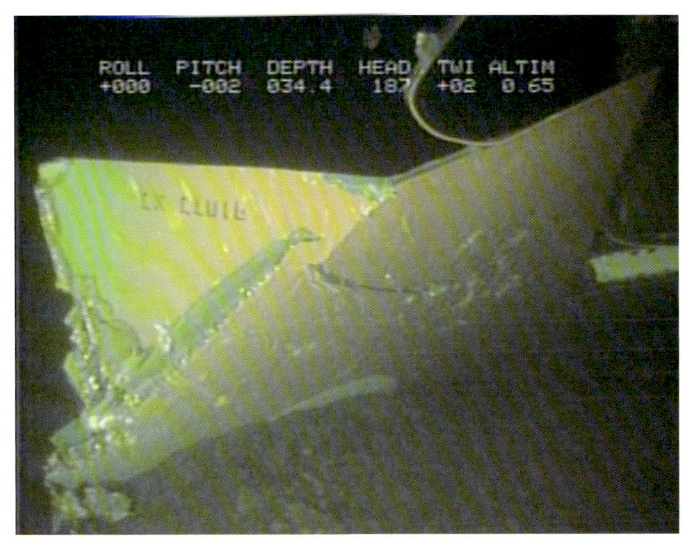

ROLL   PITCH DEPTH HEAD TWI ALTIM
+000   -002   034.4 187   +02 0.65

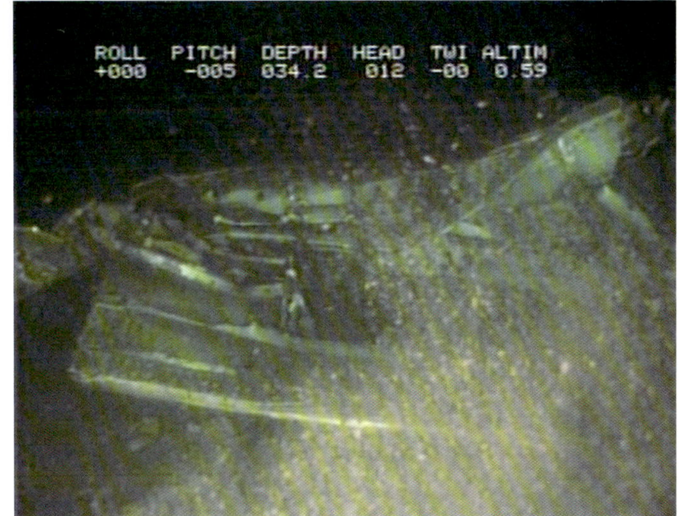

ROLL   PITCH DEPTH HEAD TWI ALTIM
+000   -005   034.2 012   -00 0.59

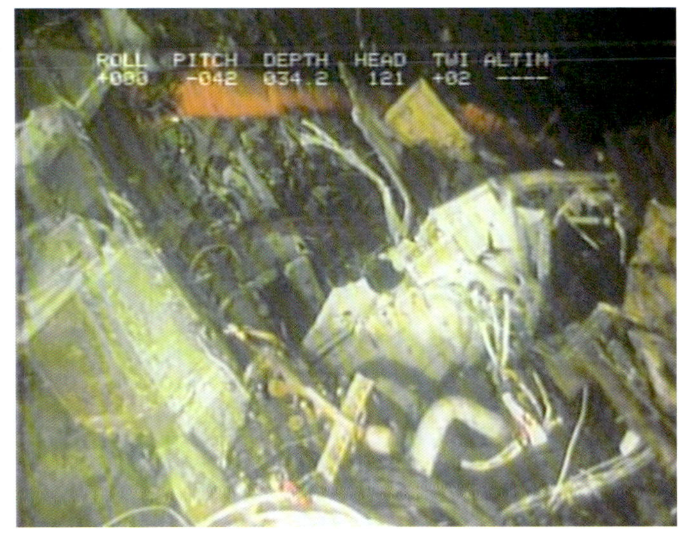

ROLL   PITCH DEPTH HEAD TWI ALTIM
+000   -042   034.2 121   +02 ----

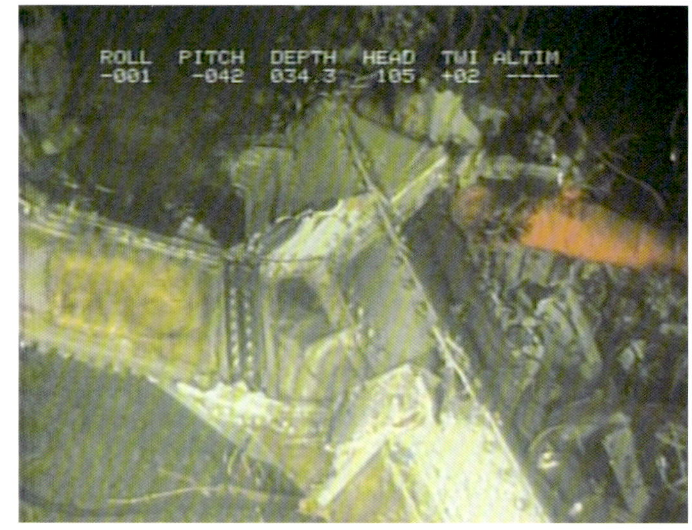

ROLL PITCH DEPTH HEAD TWI ALTIM
-001 -042   034.3 105   +02 ----

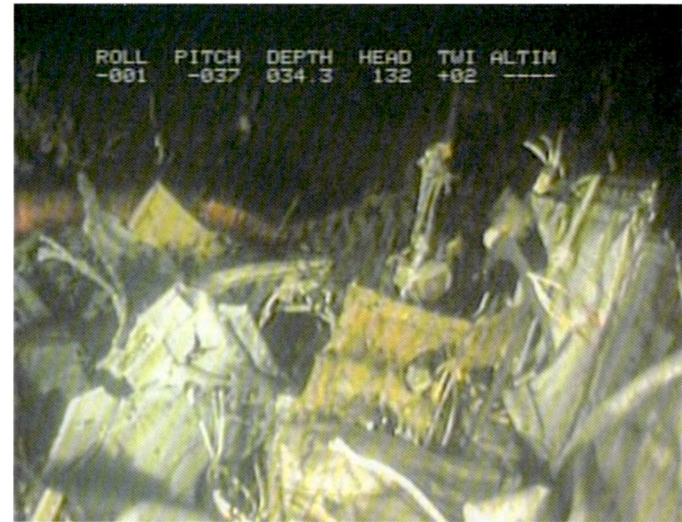

ROLL PITCH DEPTH HEAD TWI ALTIM
-001 -037   034.3 132   +02 ----

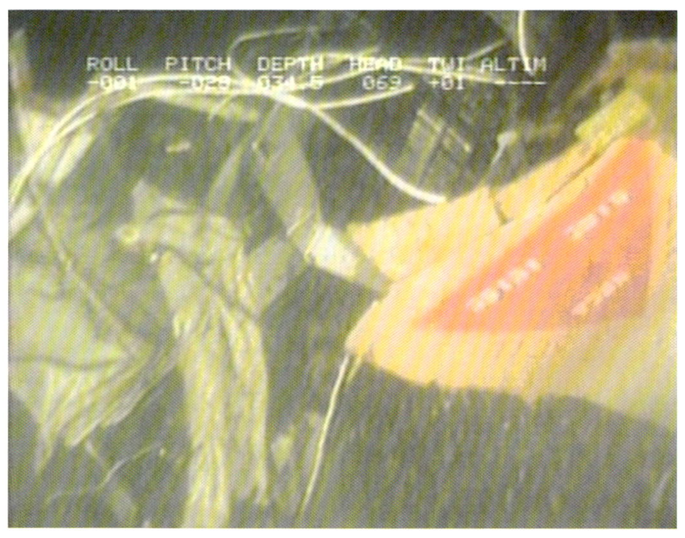

ROLL PITCH DEPTH HEAD TWI ALTIM
-001 -020   034.5 069   +01 ----

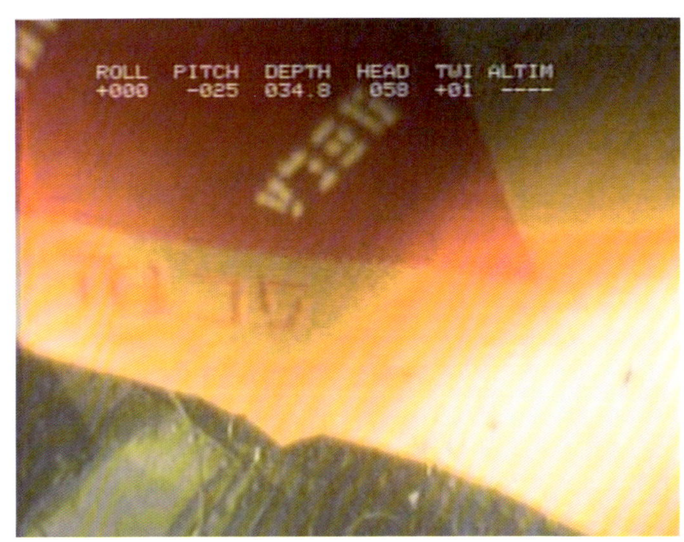

ROLL   PITCH DEPTH HEAD   TWI ALTIM
+000   -025   034.8 058   +01 ----

Phantom

2008
44 min 59 sec
Film

Von der Bewegung der ferngelenkten
Kamera mit ihrem starken Such-
licht aufgewirbelte Sandpartikel
auf Seegrund. Das Fotoauge auf
der Suche nach der Blackbox mit
den letzten Worten und nach
Wrackteilen, die gehoben werden
müssen. Silbrig leuchtend metal-
lische Einzelteile und Risse
im Rumpf der zerschellten Militär-
maschine in den Tiefen des Sees
Genezareth. „Gefahr" signalisiert
das hebräische Wort auf dem
Flügel. Die Zahlen geben die
Position an.

Bits of sand churned up by the
movement of a remote-controlled
camera with a powerful search-
light. The photographic eye
searching for the black box with
someone's last words and for
pieces of wreckage that have to
be brought up. Metallic fragments
with a silvery shine, and the
cracks in the rump of the crashed
military plane in the depths
of the Sea of Galilee. "Danger"
is signaled by the Hebrew word
on the wing. The numbers give the
position.

Runways

09   ofir

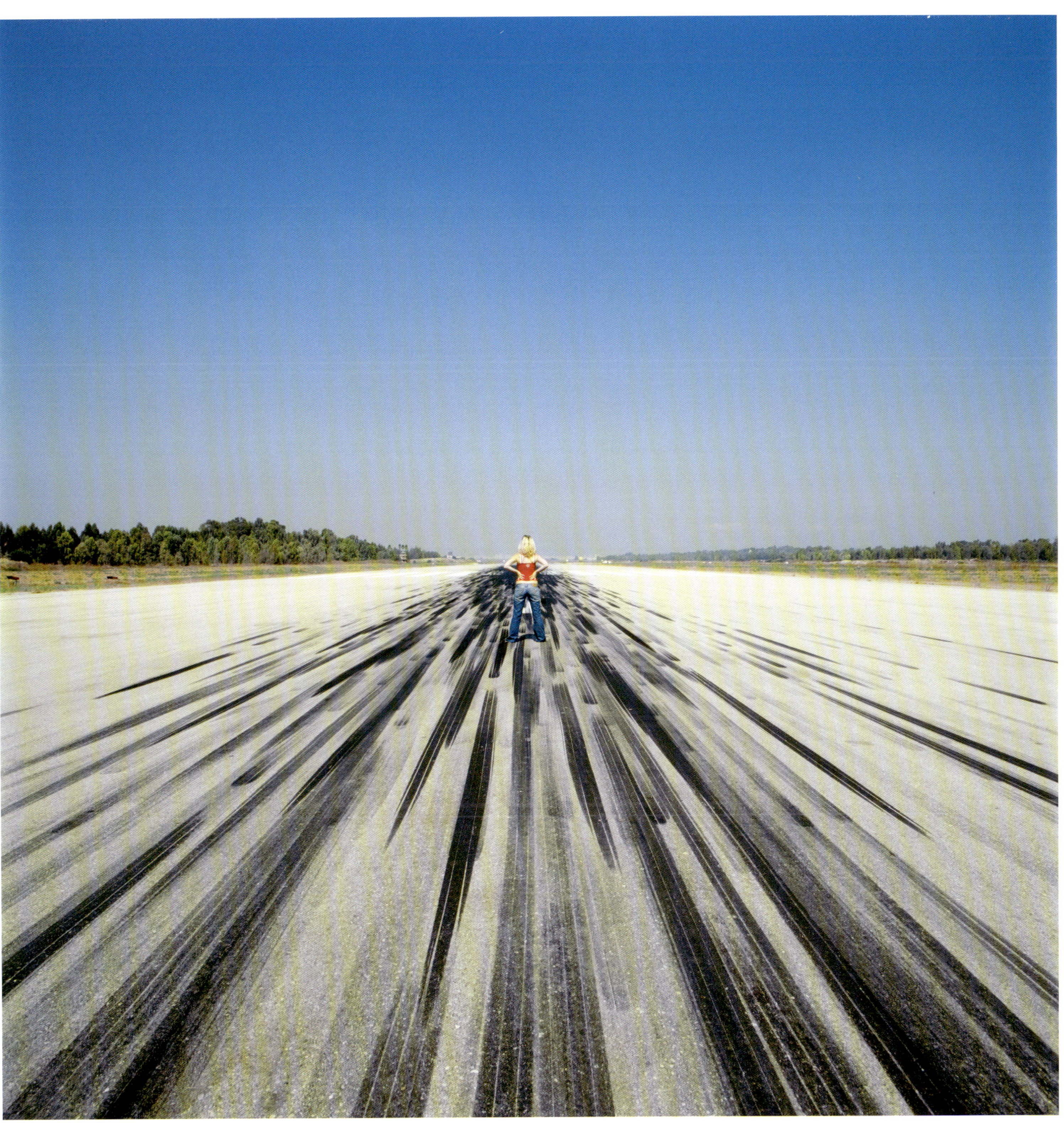

10   noa

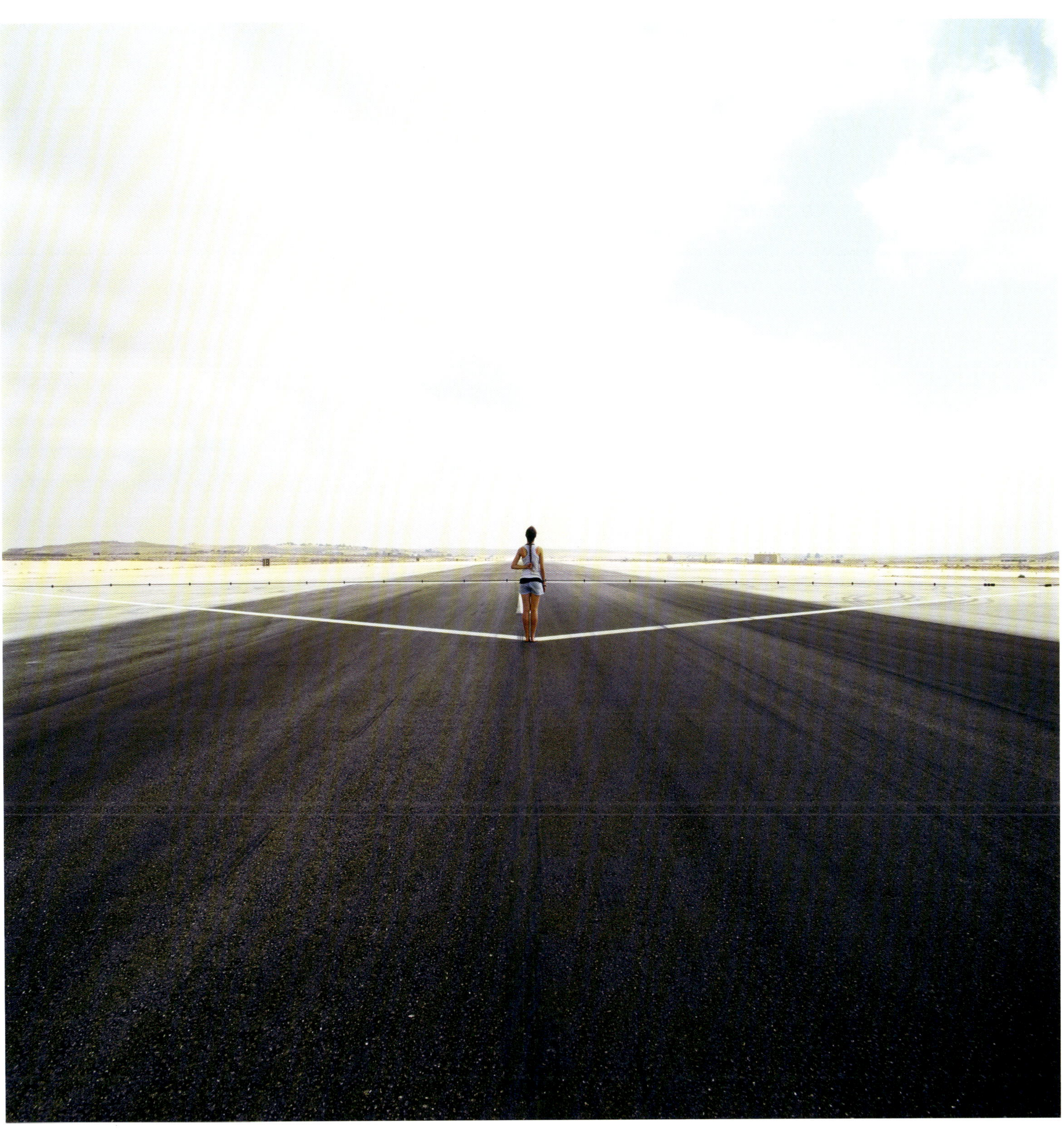

11   bar

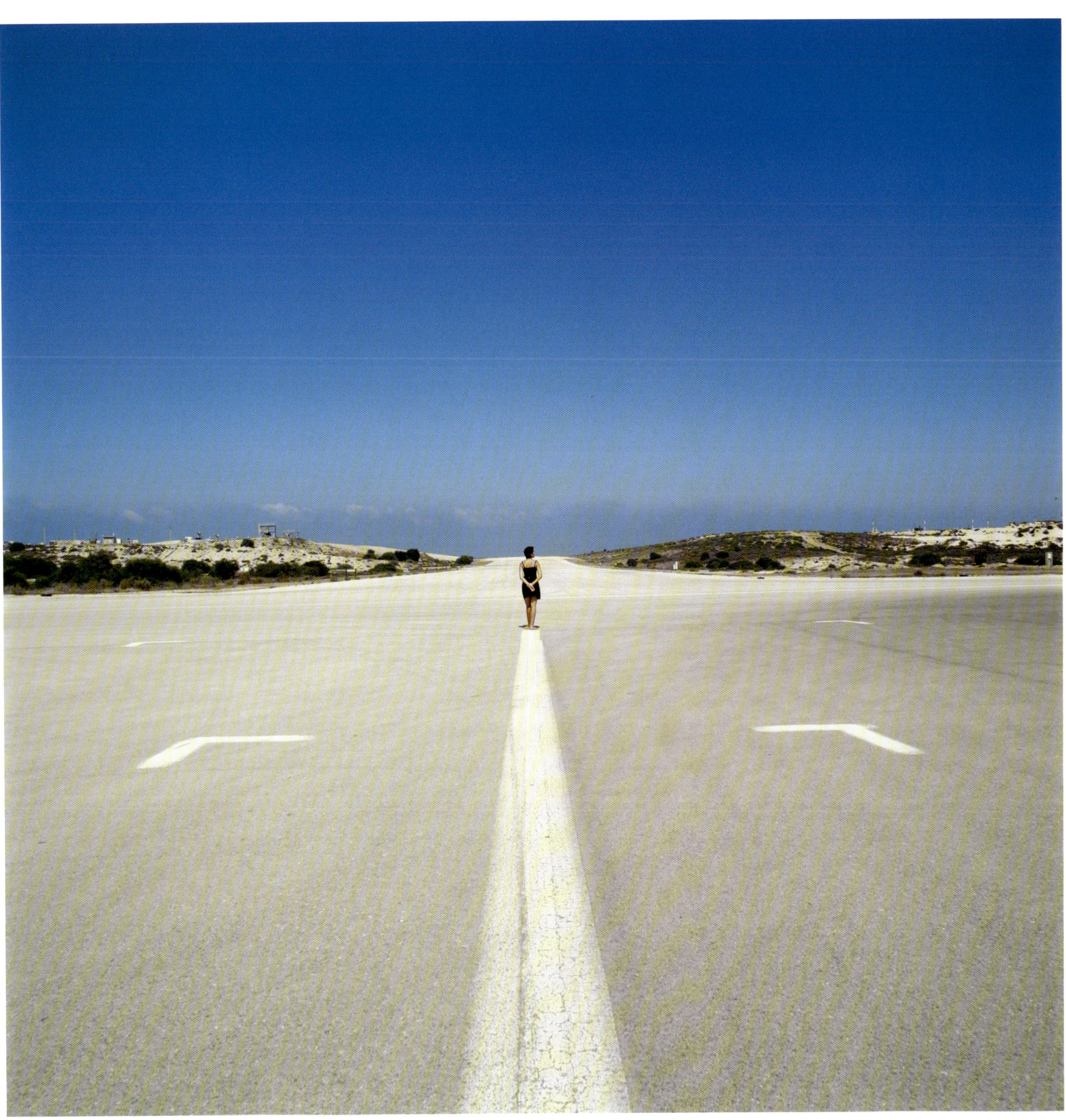

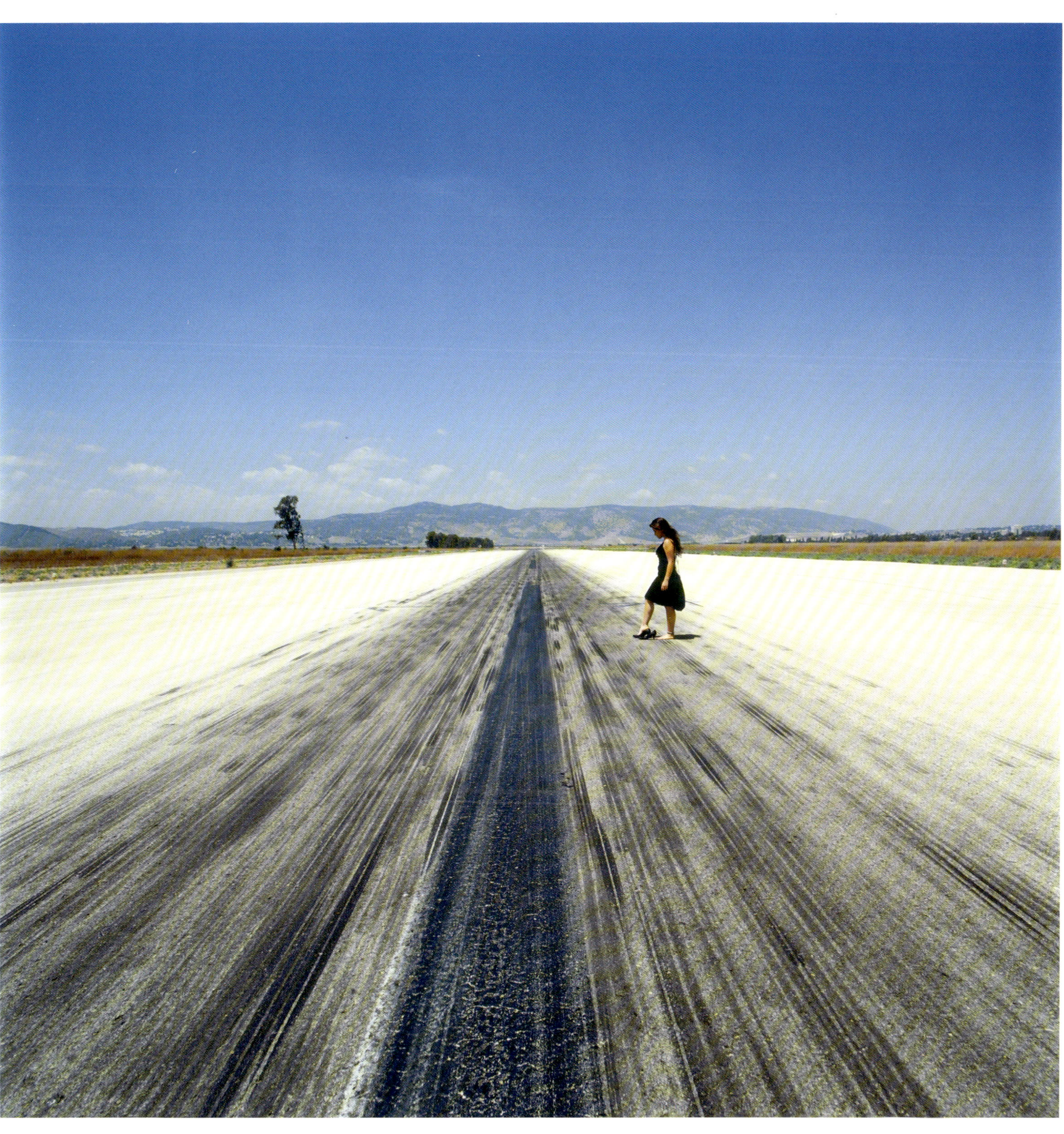

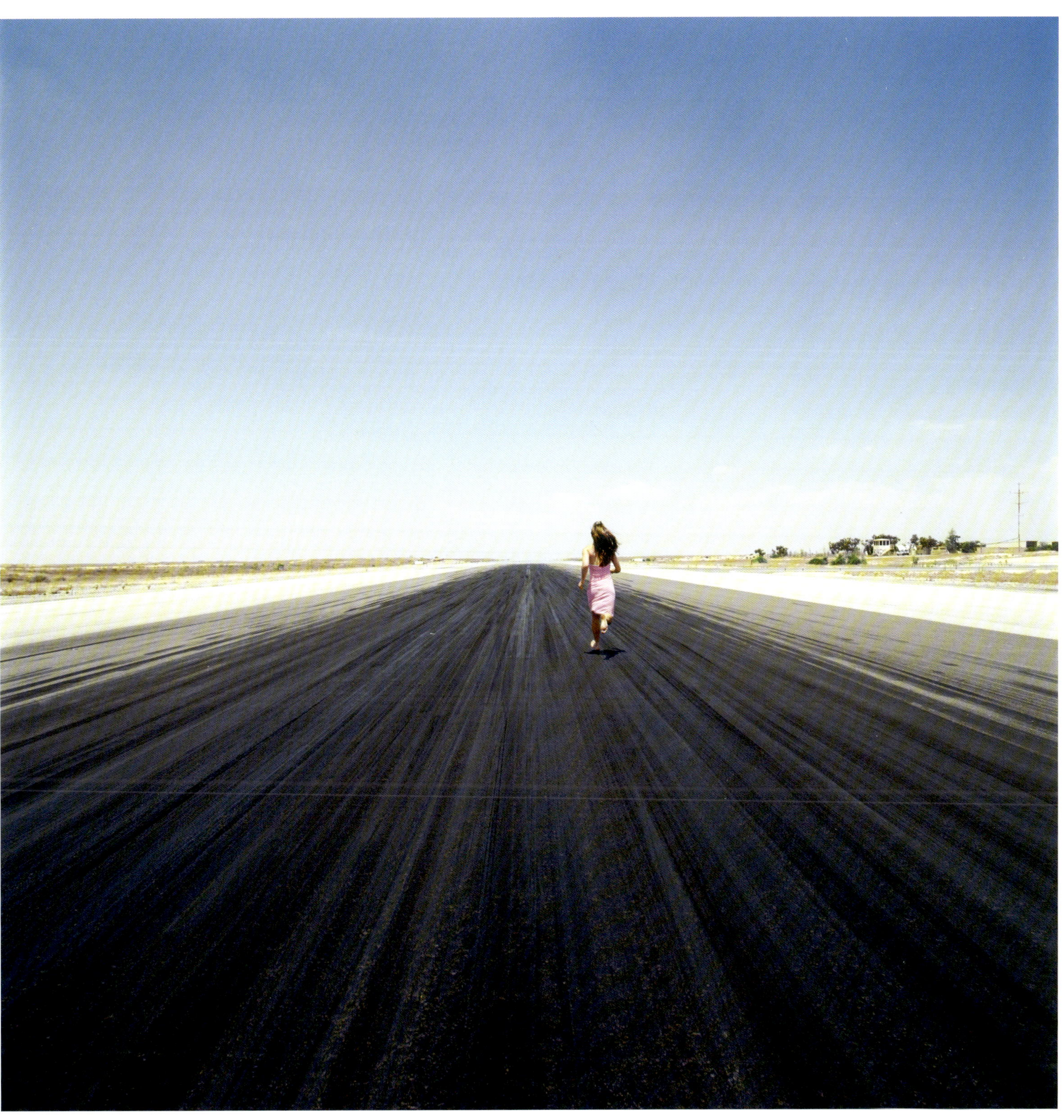

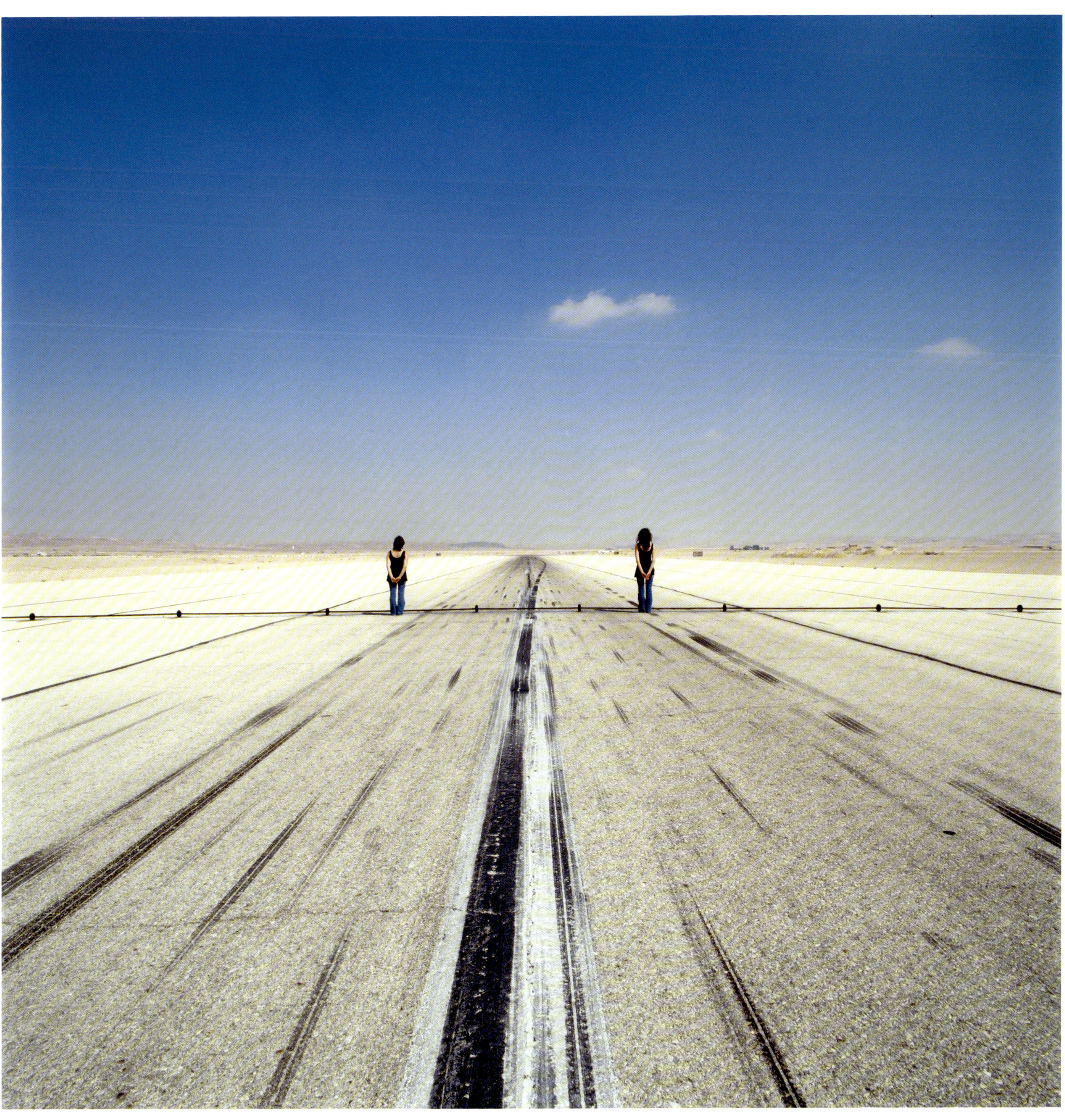

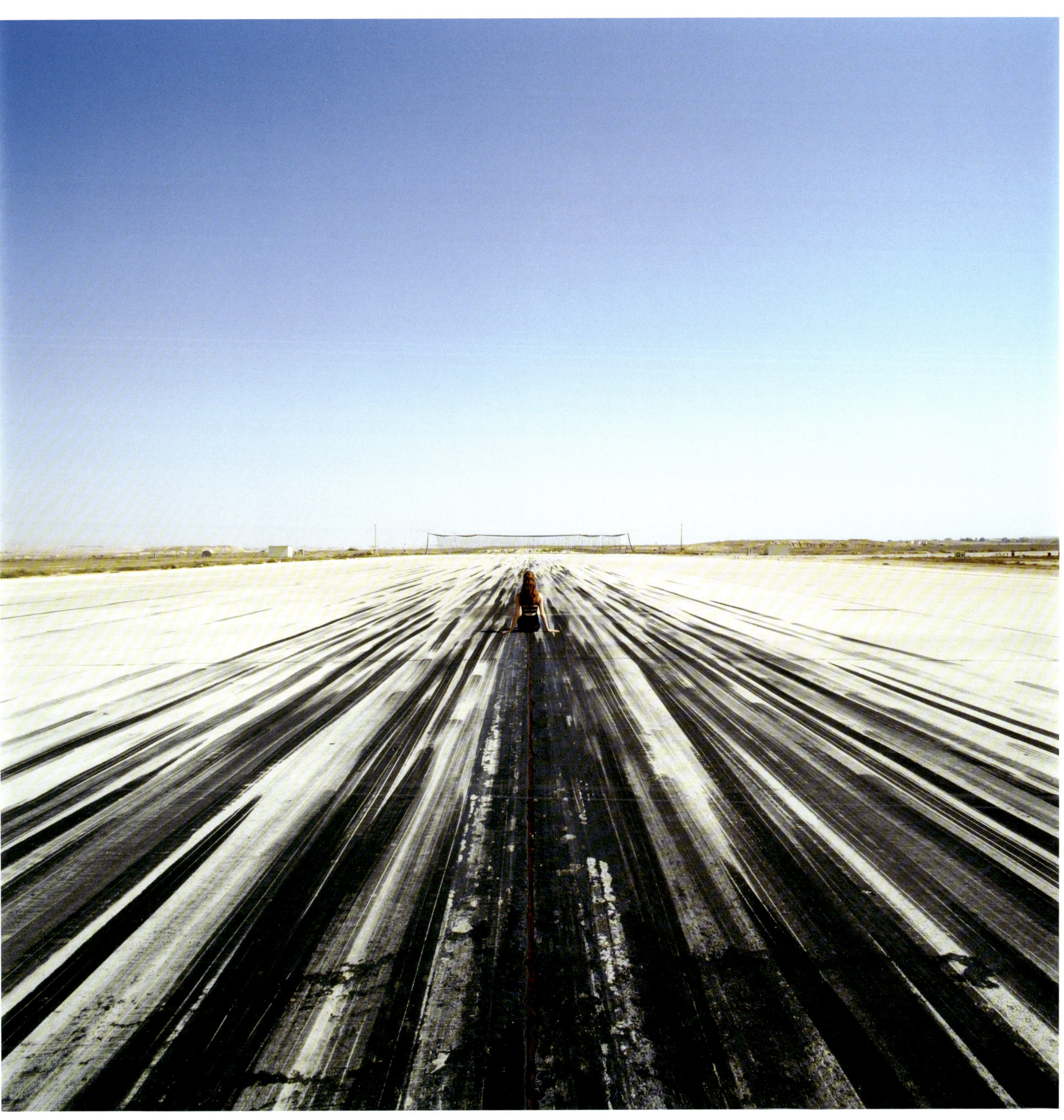

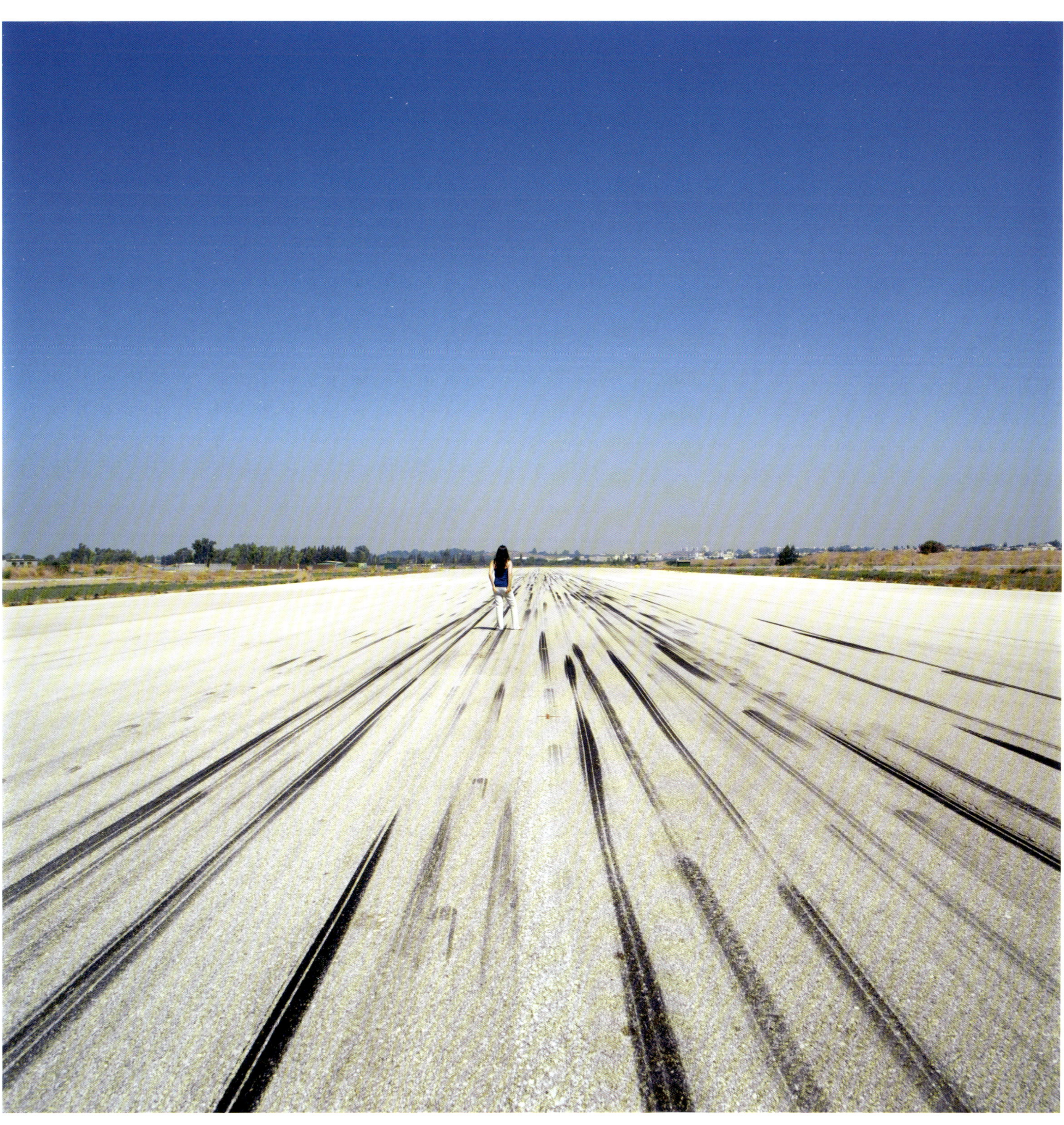

17   tal h

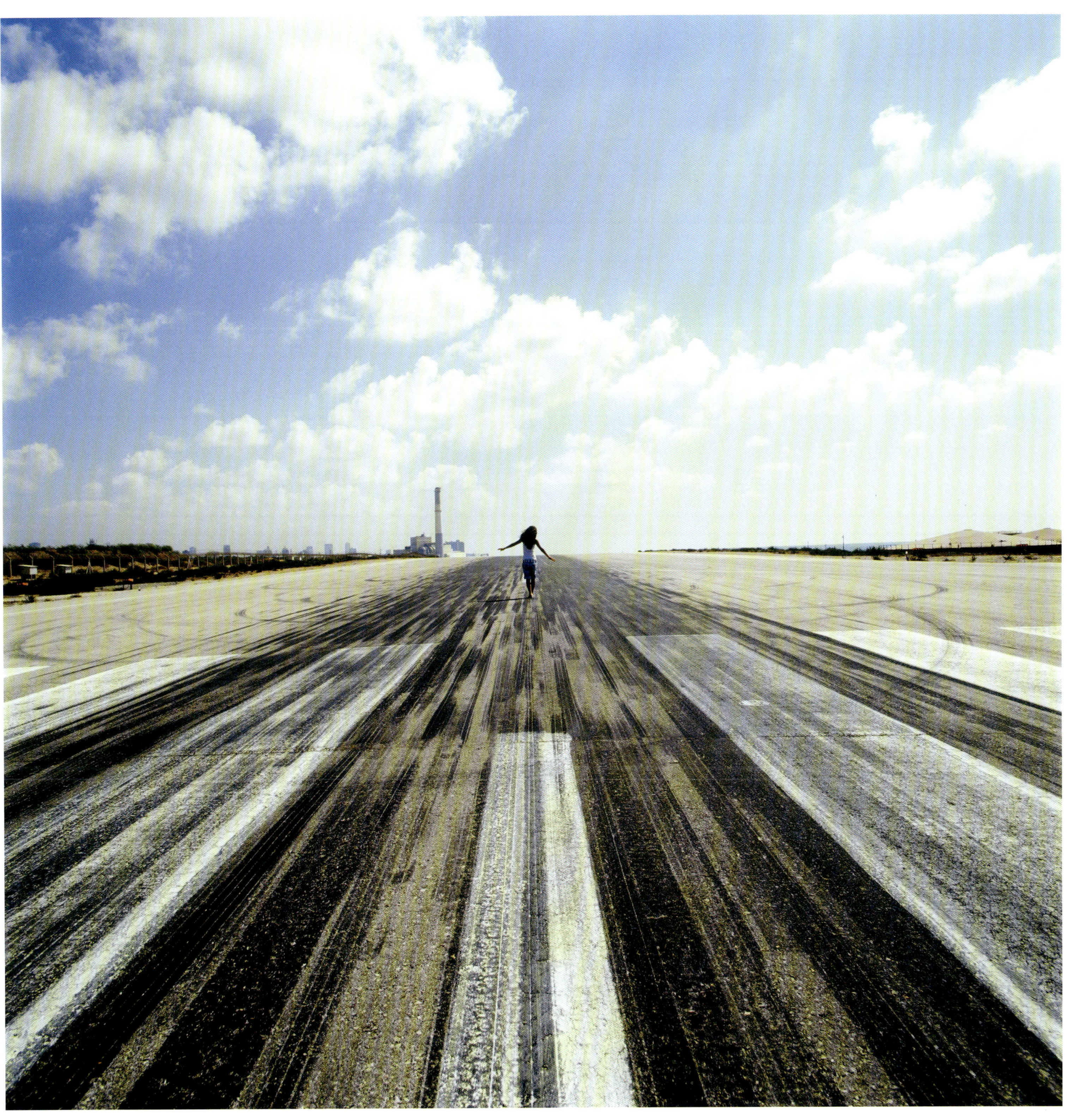

Runways

2007
je 120 cm × 120 cm
Tintenstrahlausdruck
auf Papier
auf 5 Exemplare begrenzte
Edition + einem E.A.

je 80 cm × 80 cm
c-Prints
auf 5 Exemplare begrenzte
Edition + einem E.A.

2007
each 47.24 in × 47.24 in
ink jet on fine art paper
edition of 5 + 1 a.p.

each 31.5 in × 31.5 in
c-Print
edition of 5 + 1 a.p.

Flugbasen irgendwo in Israel.
Von Bremsspuren gezeichnete Landepisten, deren Positionen nicht
benannt sein dürfen. Laufstege
junger Frauen, die demnächst ihre
obligatorische Militärdienstzeit
werden antreten müssen. Was wird
sein? Letzte Tage der farbigen
Alltagsfreiheit vor dem Tag, an
der sie ihre Uniform fassen. Eine
ungewisse Zeit vor ihnen, so un-
sicher wie jeder Abflug der don-
nernden Militärjets, die von hier
aus zu ihren Missionen starten und
wieder unter Höllenlärm landen.

Air bases somewhere in Israel.
Skid-marked airstrips whose
locations are kept secret.
Runways for young women who will
soon have to start their obligatory military service. What is
going to happen? The final days
of colorful freedom before the day
when they will put on their uni-
forms. An uncertain time ahead,
as uncertain as each takeoff of the
thundering military jets starting
their missions here and landing
again in a frenzy of noise.

Lizette

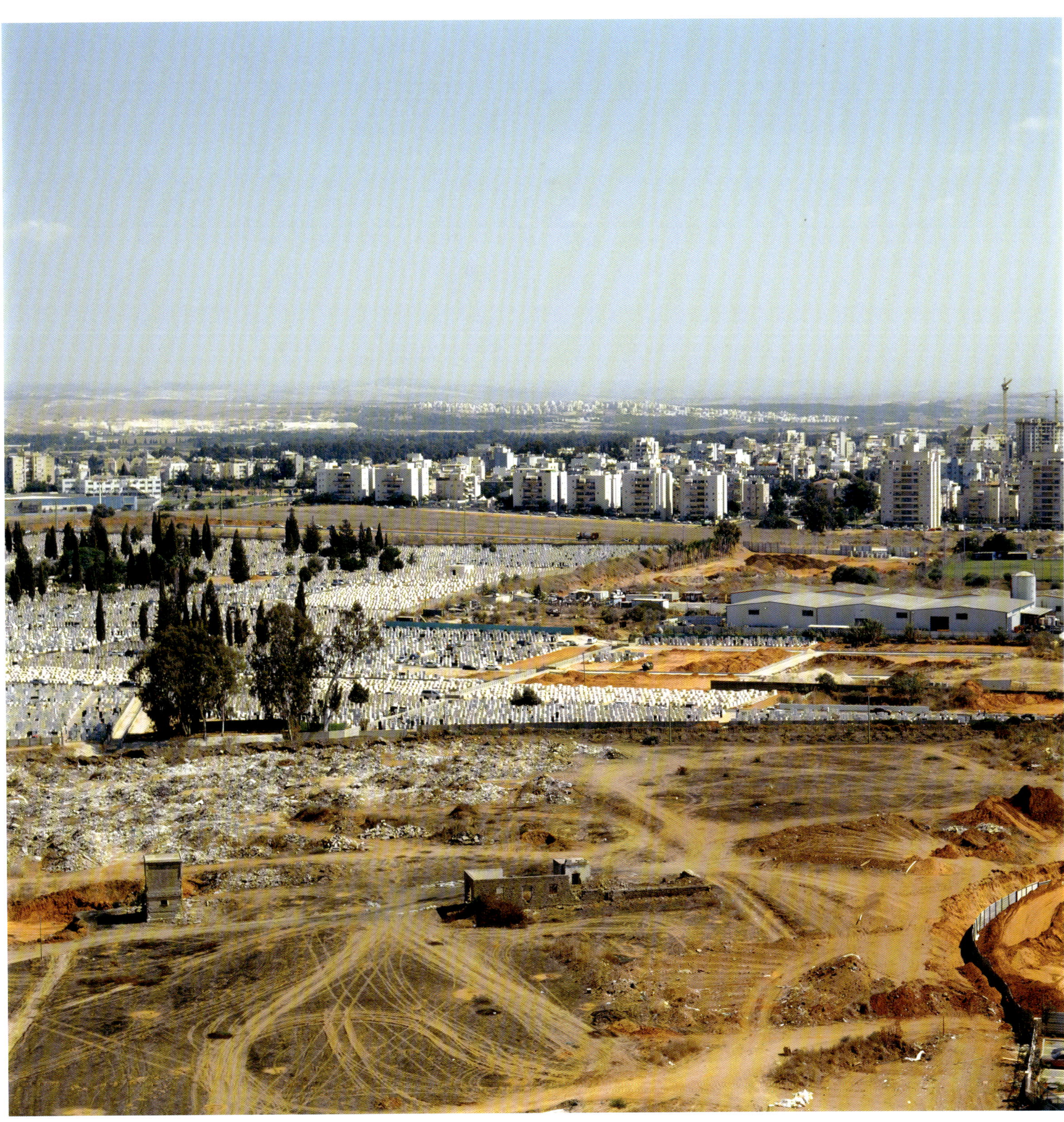

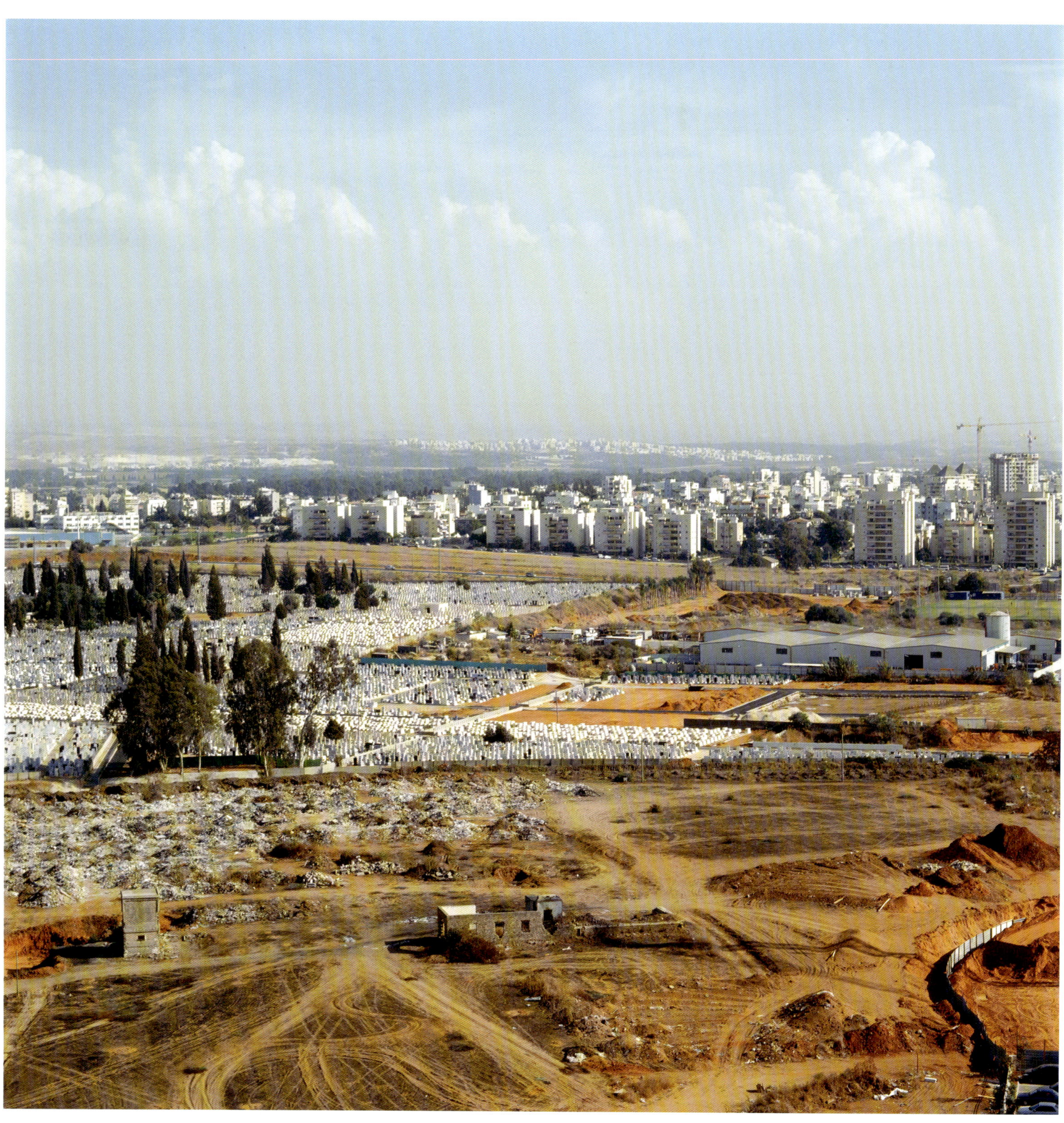

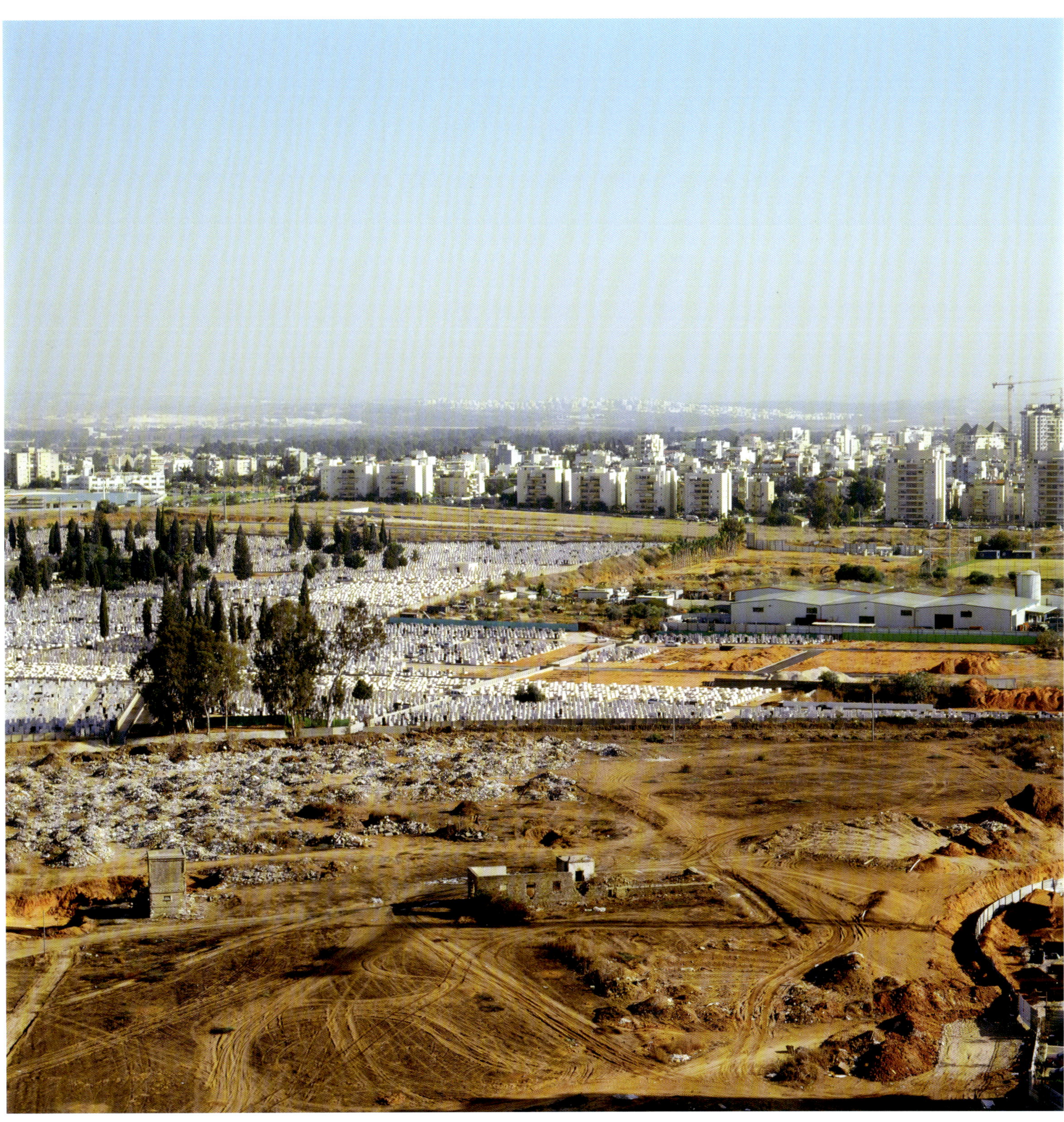

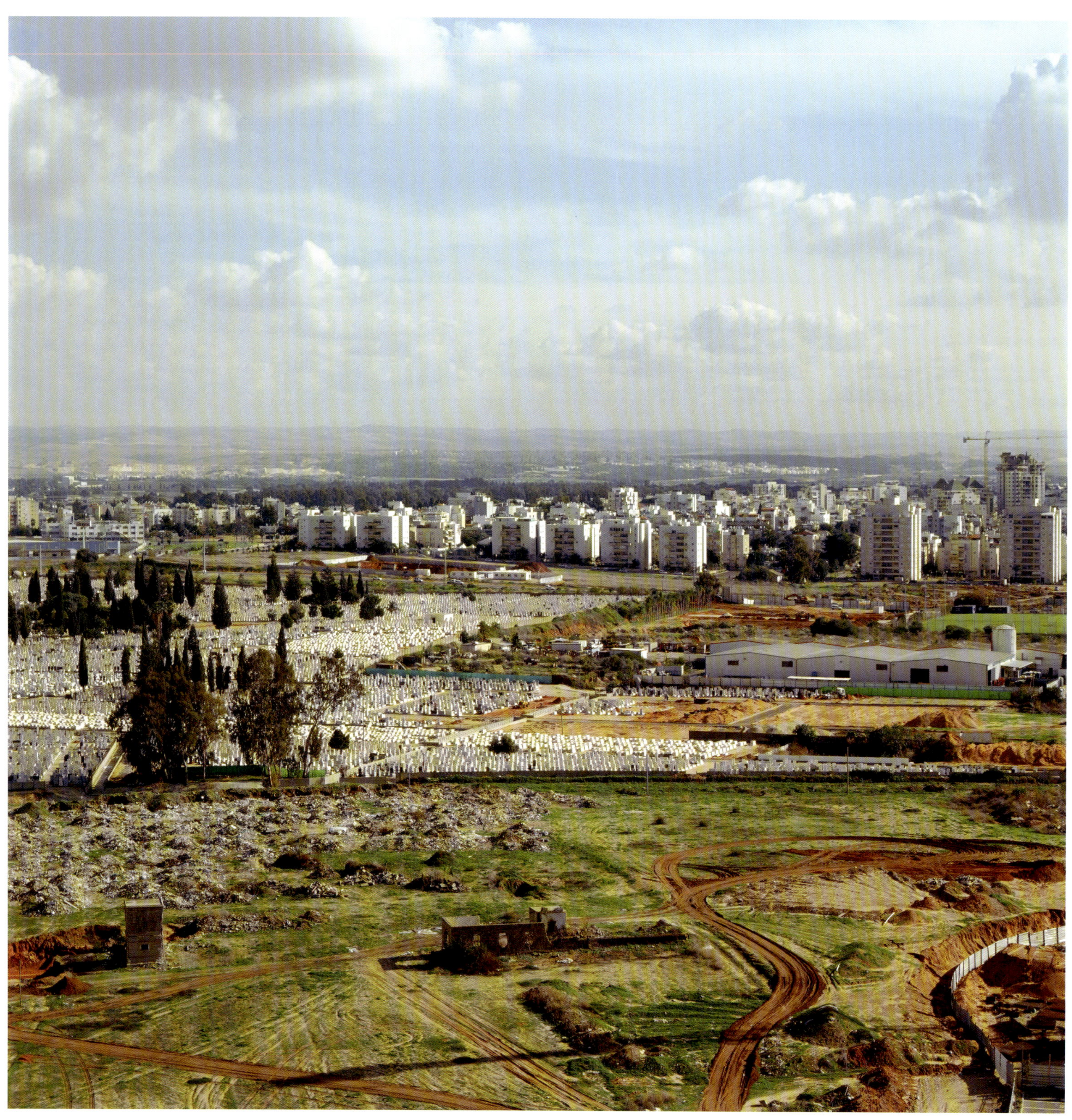

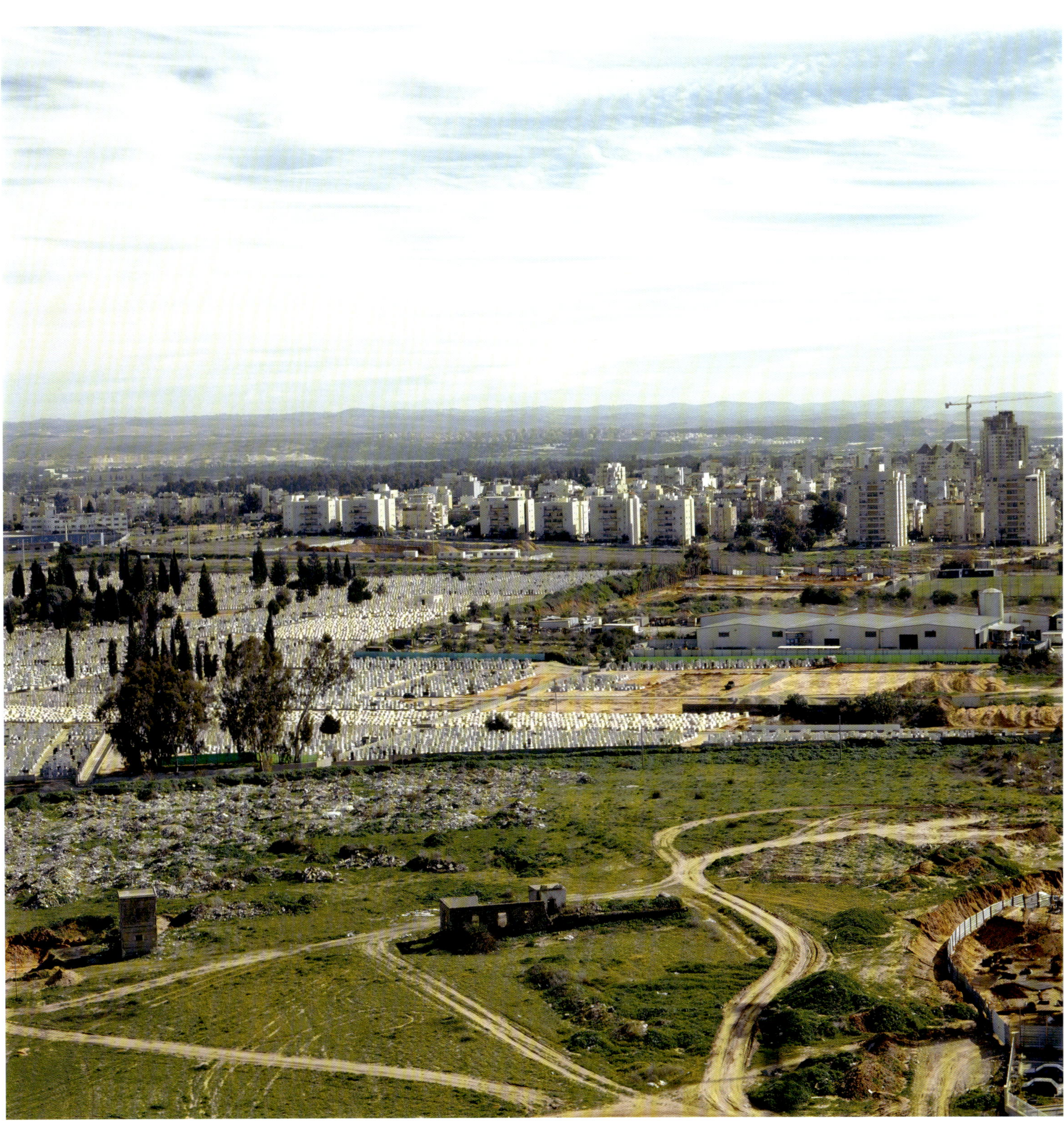

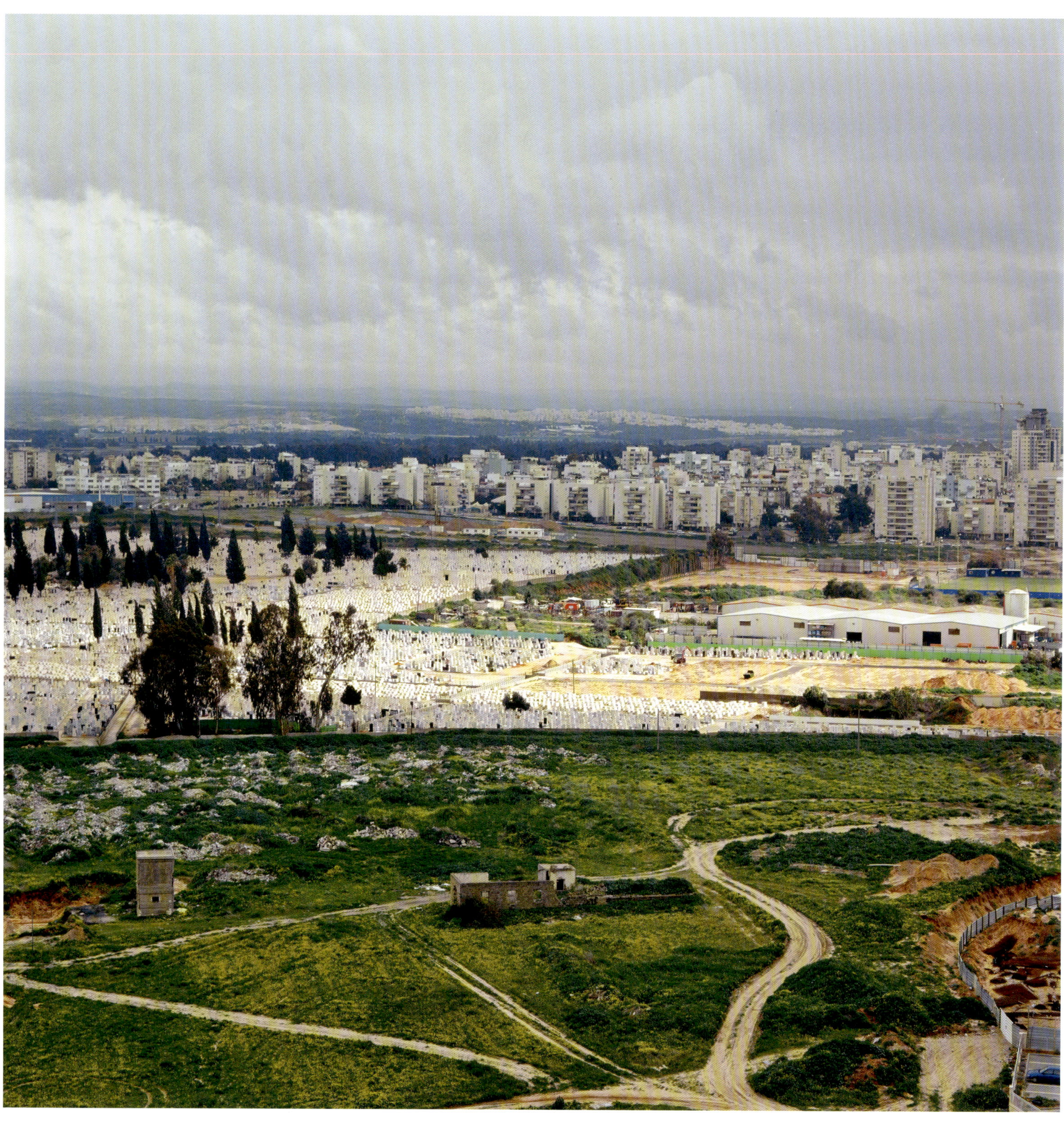

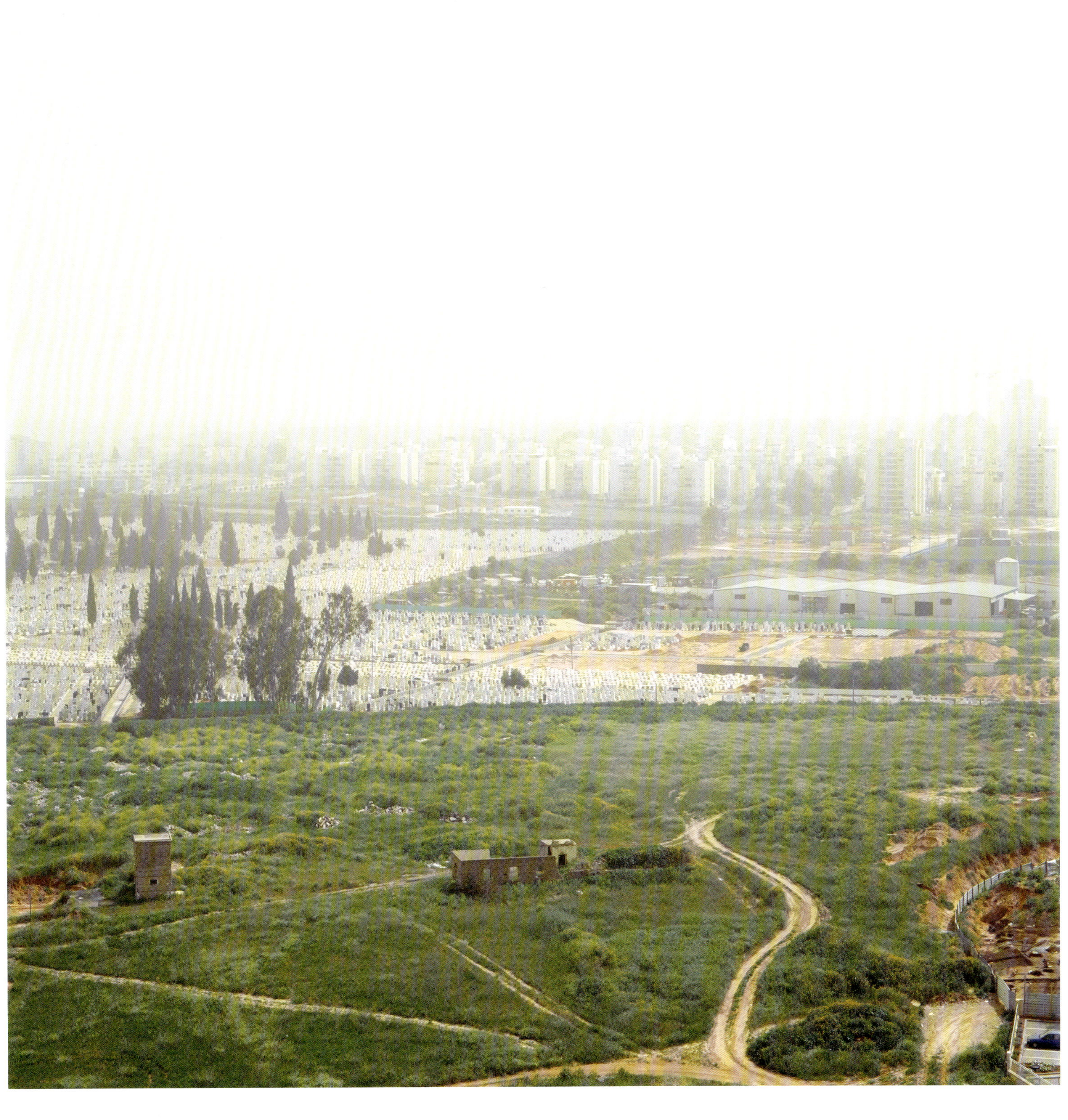

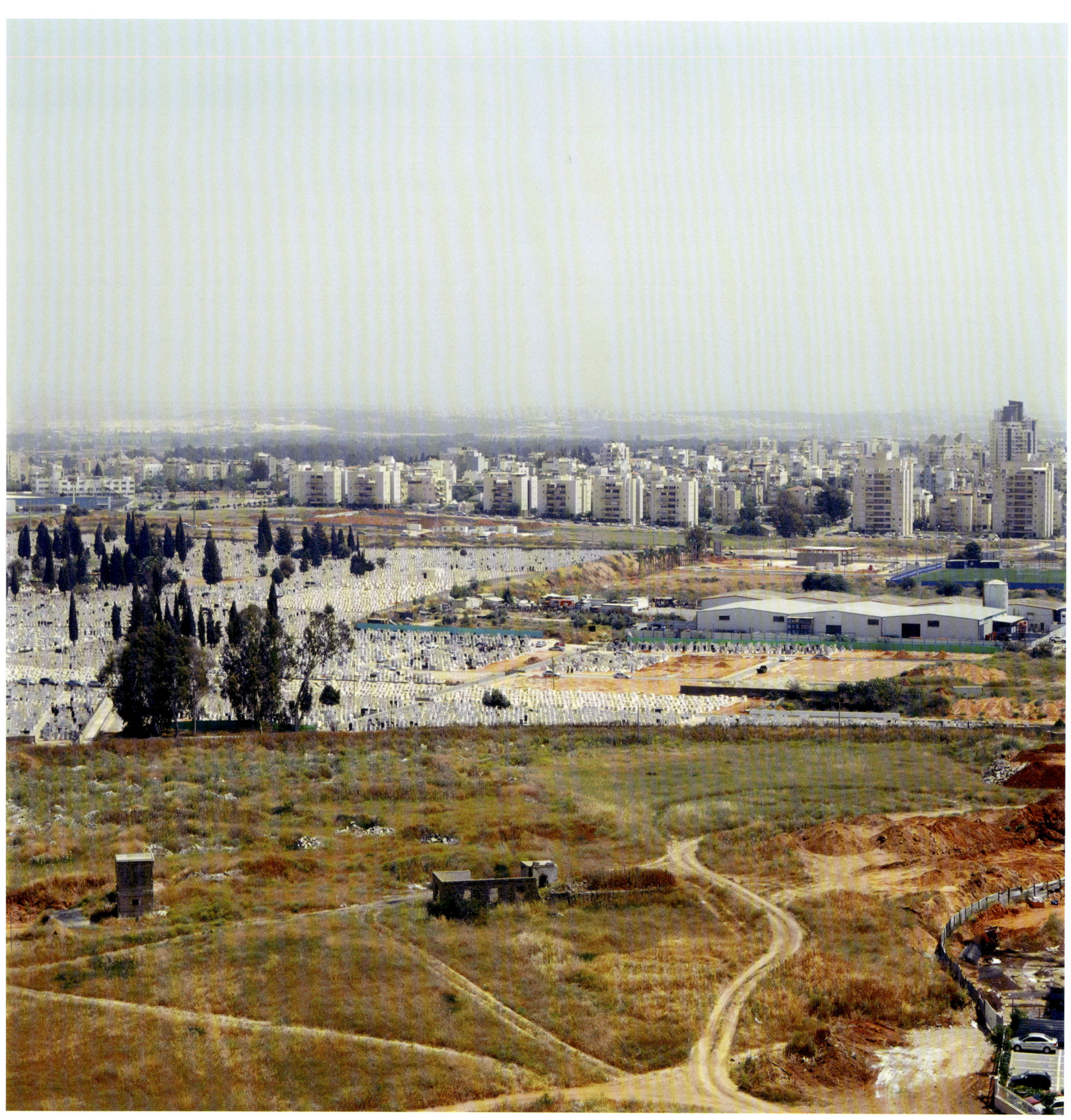

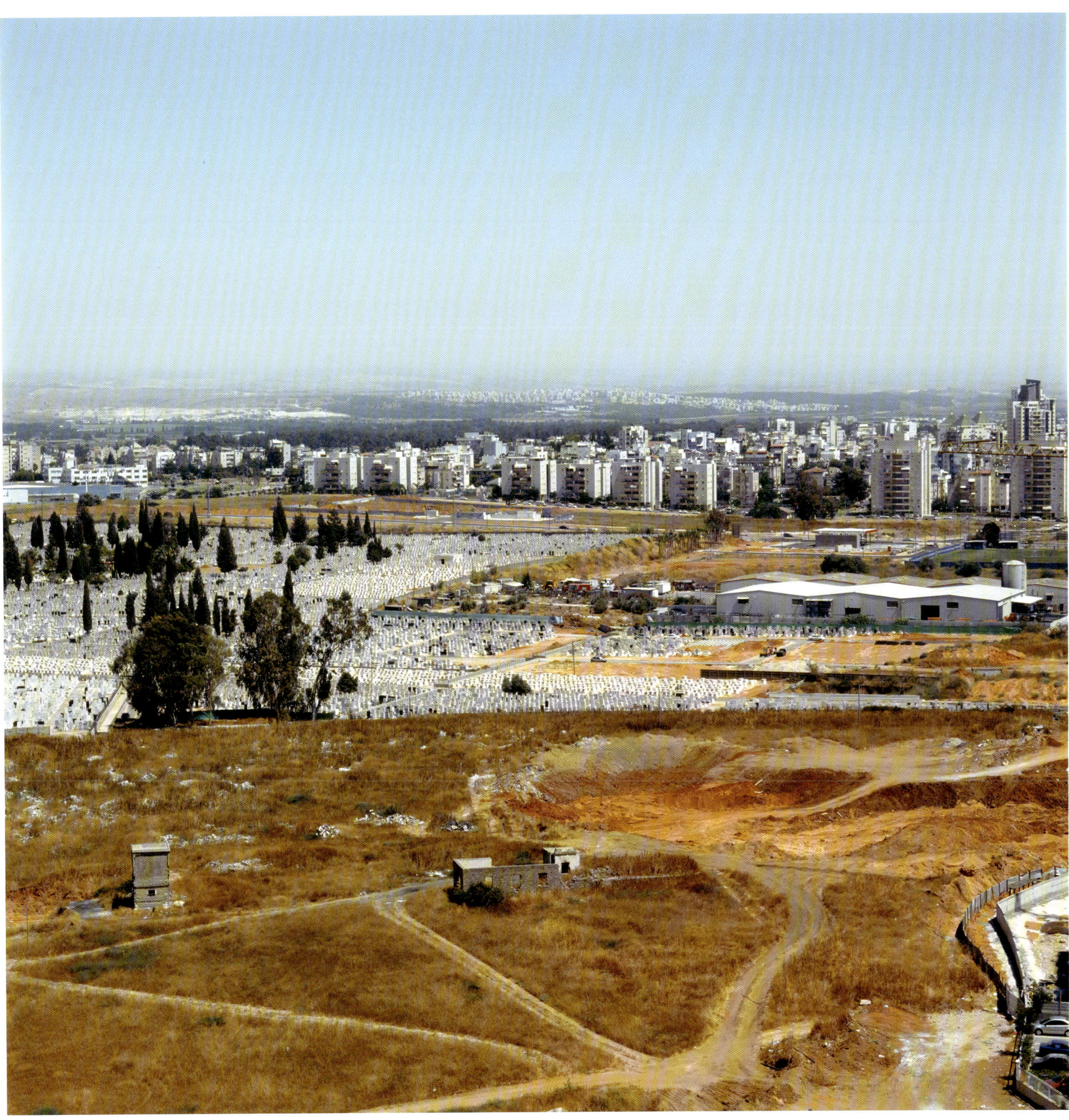

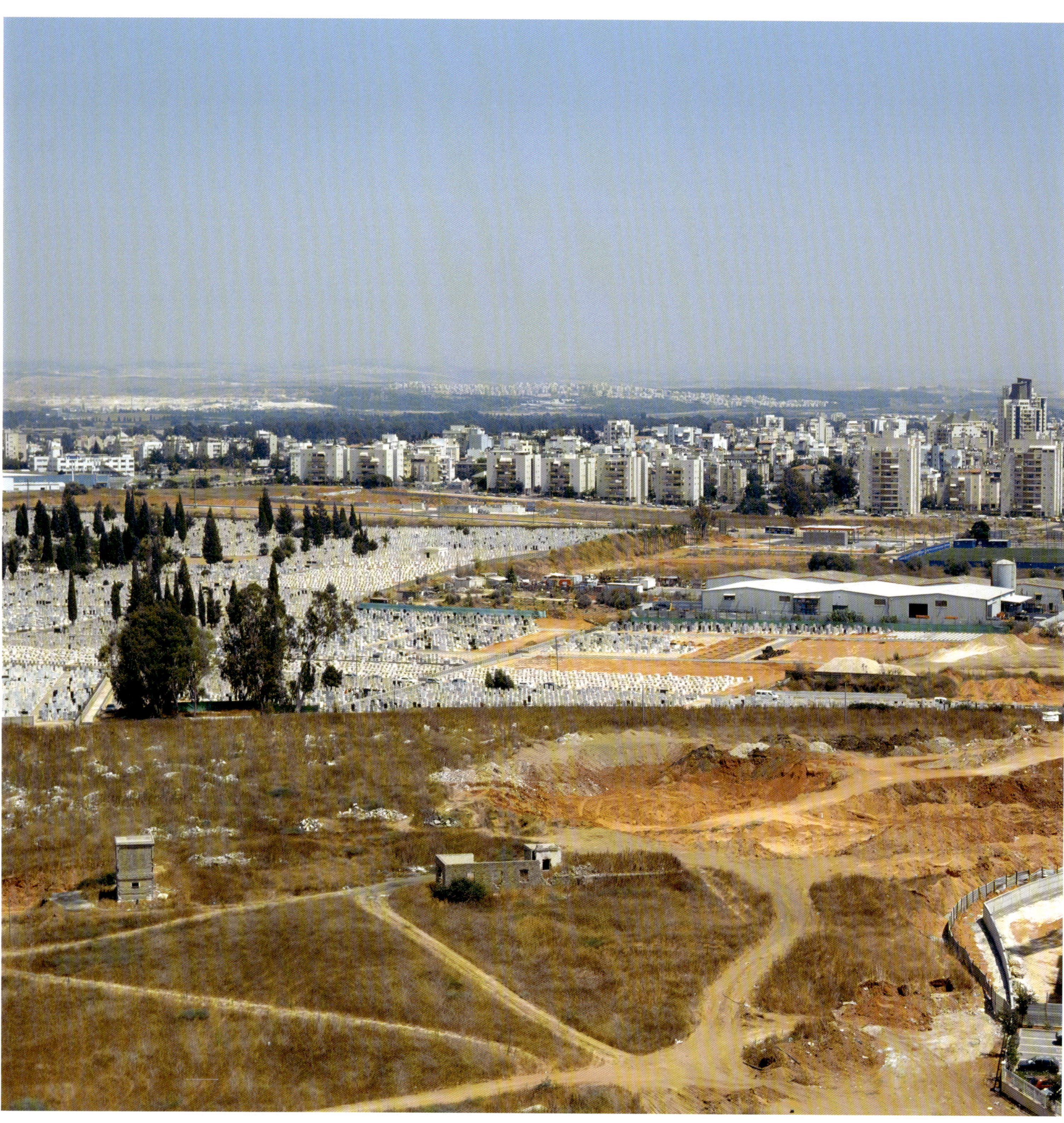

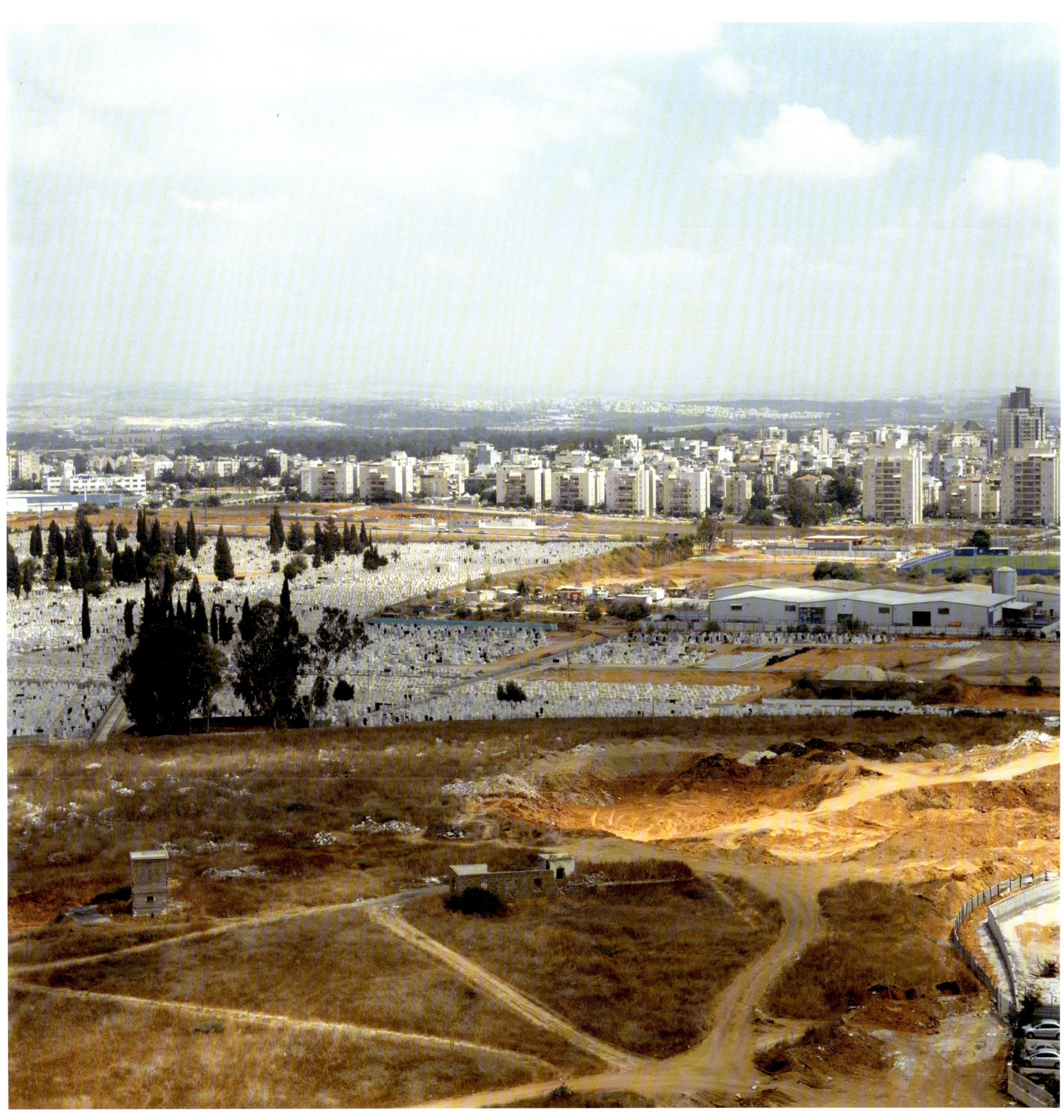

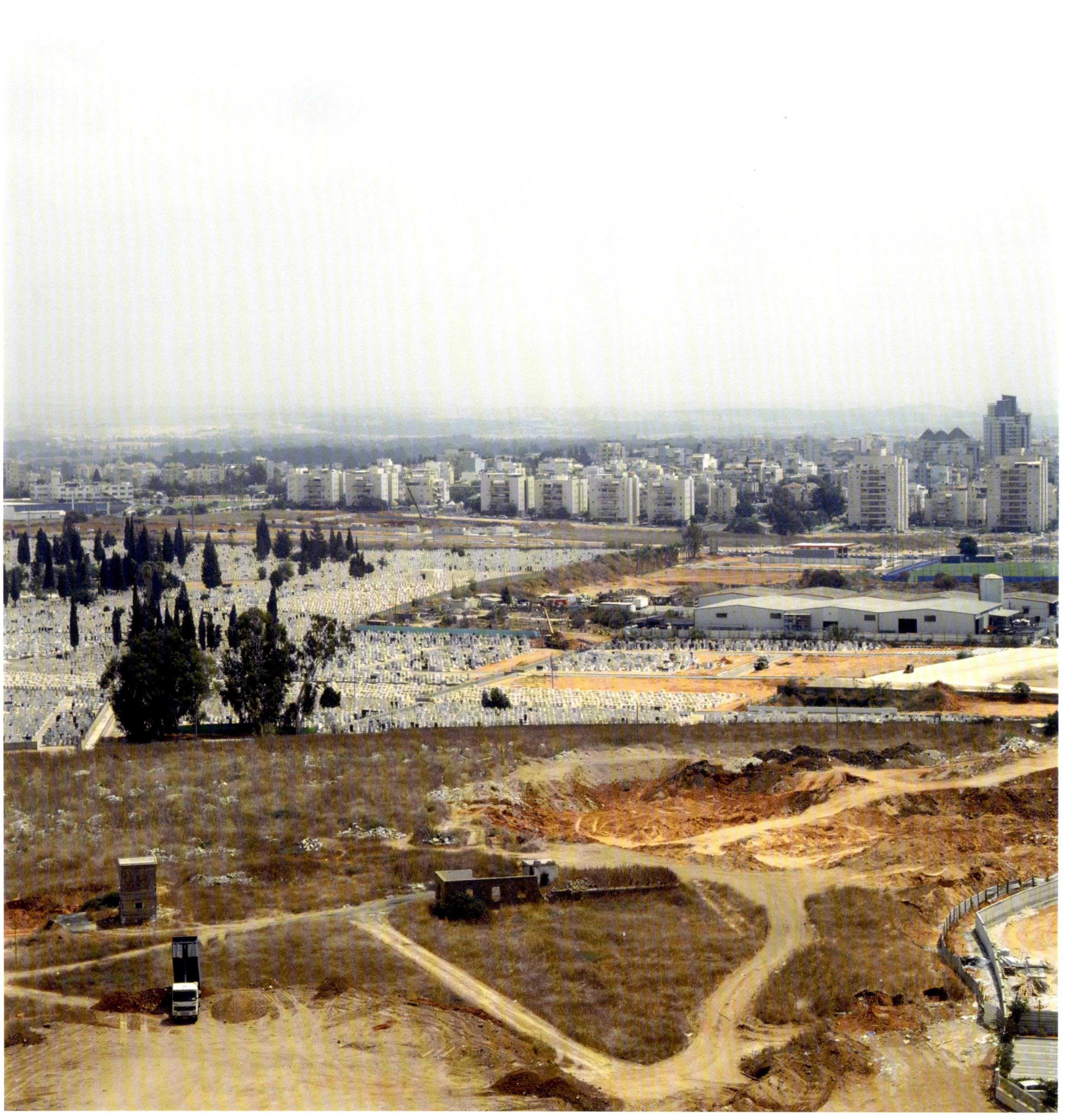

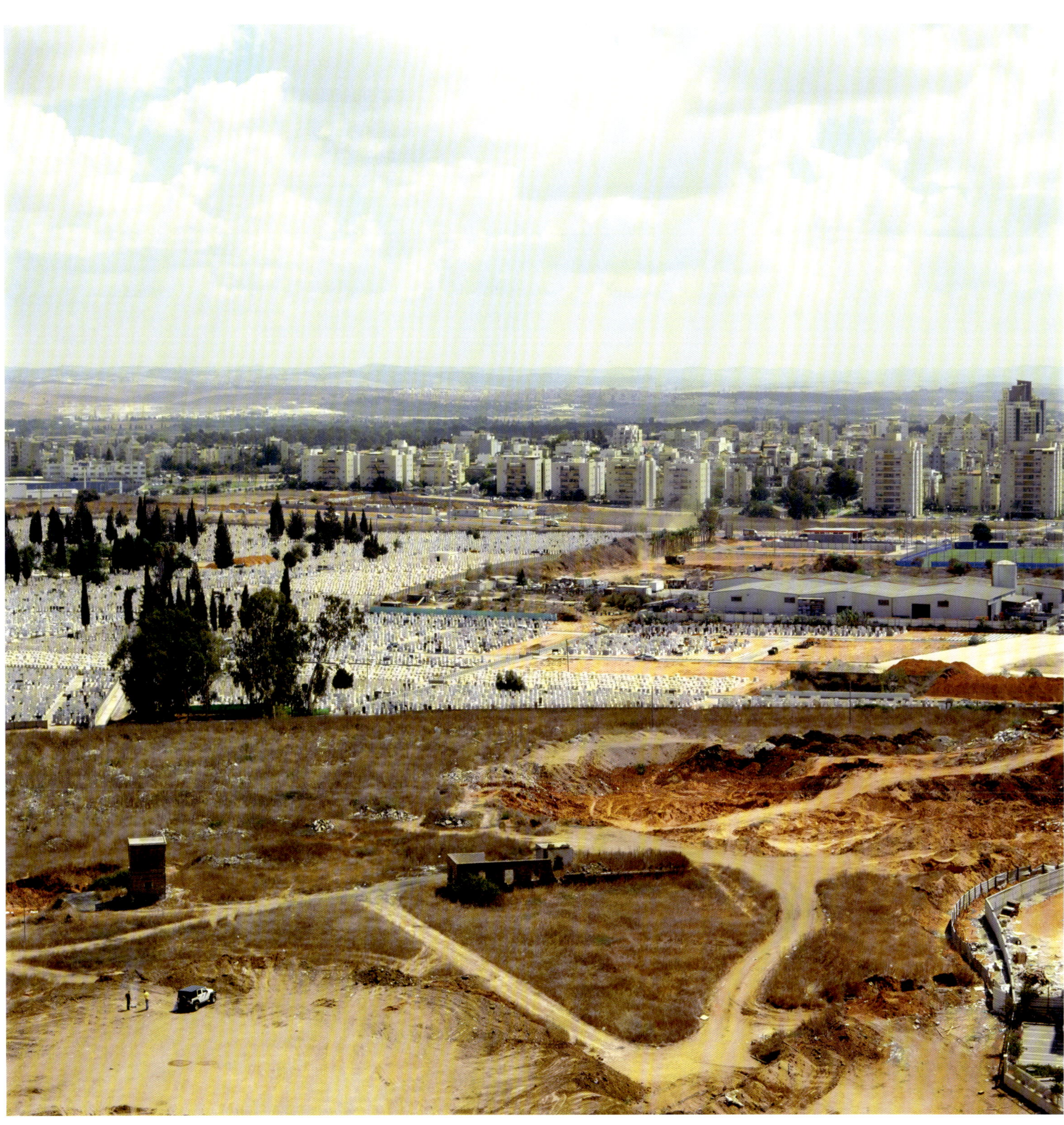

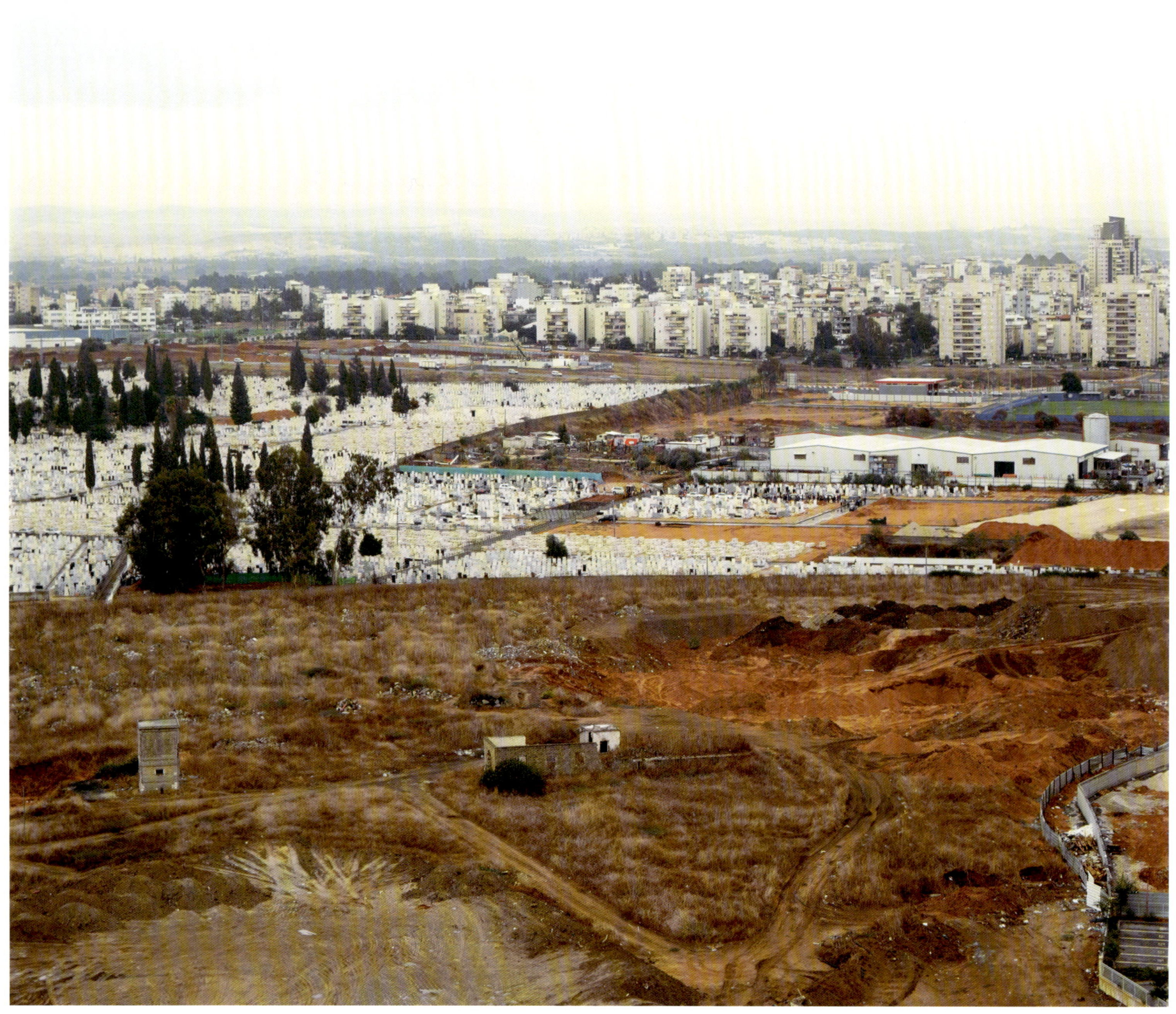

Lizette

2007 / 2008
je 50 cm x 50 cm
c-Prints
auf 5 Exemplare begrenzte
Edition + einem E.A.

2007 / 2008
each 19.69 in × 19.69 in
c-Print
edition of 5 + 1 a.p.

Mittagsbilder. Jeden Monat eine
Fotografie vom selben Ort aus
in dieselbe Richtung aufgenommen.
Wenn die ersten grossen Regen im
Dezember übers Land fegen, wird
die sonnentrockene Erde grün und
der zwischen zwei Siedlungen
gelegene Friedhof ist um einige
weisse Grabsteine weiter ange-
wachsen. Leuchtend grün der März
im Mittagsnebel, sonnenverbrannt
die karge Erde in den Sommer-
monaten Juni und Juli.

Midday pictures. Every month,
a photograph taken from the same
spot, in the same direction.
When the first great rains of
December blow across the land,
the sun-dried earth turns green
and the cemetery that lies
between two housing developments
will have more white gravestones.
The shining green of March in
midday haze, the barren earth
burned by the sun in the summer
months of June and July.

Was zusammenhält

Tiefes und wärmendes Blau koloriert die Aura der heiligen Landschaft. Ein Fischerboot ruht auf dem morgendlichen Spiegel des Sees Genezareth. Das Vorspiel, betitelt mit „Way to beyond", öffnet einleitend die ganze Breite von Kontinuität und Stabilität, erzählt von göttlicher und poetischer Stimmung. Himmel, Frieden, Traum und Sehnsucht leuchten als Farbklänge auf. Ultramarin führt den spirituellen Raum des Jordangrabens in die sanften Übergänge zu den Hügeln Galiläas weiter. Textbilder aus dem Testament werden in diesem ätherischen Kraftraum wahrhaftig und hörbar, Erzählungen von Ereignissen und Ewigkeit. Geheiligtes Land und Fischgewässer sind Territorium, sinnliches wie metaphorisches Futteral, in das uns Naomi Leshem einbettet. Die Fotografin empfängt uns in einer geführten, kontemplativen Stille. Die Wahl dieser idealen Landschaft als Auftakt des vierteiligen Zyklus bleibt vorerst noch Geheimnis.

„Phantom" bricht mit der blauen Stille der Landschaft und rückt Katastrophe in die Welt. Mit allen fotografischen und filmischen Mitteln binden Videobilder die Wirklichkeit an den Tod. Der Tod ist nun selbst Hauptdarsteller und Gegengewicht von Leben. Trümmerschneisen auf dem Seegrund von Genezareth sind die Wegstationen der Suchbilder. Keine Horizonte existieren mehr. Die Orte sind aufgelöst. Die rechte Flügelspitze soll es gewesen sein, die im Blendlicht den Spiegel des Sees touchierte. Zuwendung wie Abkehr lösen sich ab. Die Sprache beginnt wie die Schärfe des Blicks zu verschwimmen. Willkürlich und collagenartig ordnen sich die Stills aus militärischen Videos in Zeugnisblöcken als Botschafter des Todes. Keine Stimmen sprechen hier und der Tod erscheint als Raum. Schal und dumpf sind die Farben im Richtungswechsel suchender Scheinwerfer. Ein Roboter mit Kamera tastet sich über dem Seegrund vor. Er verlangsamt bei Unsicherheit der Wahrnehmung, beschleunigt in unbesetztem Gelände. Überall will er finden und gewinnen. Zwischen den bewegten Wolken aufgewühlter Sedimente liegen die stummen Wrackteile des zerborstenen Kampfjets. Es sind Spuren einer chaotischen, tödlichen Topografie und dennoch als Spuren von Flugtechnik Botschaften vom Diesseits. Wir sind Zeugen einer Archäologie des Auseinanderbrechens, der Zerstörung, der Registrierung von Wrackteilen, die keine

Klärung für das Leben mehr bringen. Zuwendung wechselt immer in Abwendung. Alles nur noch Argumente für den Tod.

Die stille und meditative Sprache der Bilder in den „Runways" wagt die Kehrtwendung von dem, was geschehen und in „Phantom" dokumentiert ist. Licht, Farbe und Wärme weiten die fernen Horizonte. Himmel und Erde haben sich und halten starke Gegenwart. Unsere Blicke erfahren eine starke Bündelung. Sie überspringen in streng geführten Richtungen Start- und Landebahnen, Kreuzungen, Querungen, Markierungen, Auffangnetze. Die RWY (Runways) existieren im Sog des Fernblicks und existieren zugleich nicht. Die guten Wetterverhältnisse entsprechen den Sichtflugregeln VFR (Visual Flight Rules), doch sind die ohrenbetäubenden und todbringenden Kampfjets wie von Geisterhand weggezaubert. Auch die erwarteten Schnittmuster von Kondensstreifen am Himmelszelt finden sich nirgendwo. Reinheit und Stille sind eingekehrt. Doch die zunehmende Gewissheit um die Standorte nährt auch hier das Bewusstsein einer grossen Illusion. Wir stehen mit der Fotografin innerhalb der Landeschwellen, da wo kein Sterblicher steht, sich hinbewegen darf. Unrast, Bedrohung und Verunsicherung rücken uns feindlich oder doch sehr bedrohlich entgegen. Ruppig haben sich die grob hingeklatschten Reifenabriebe pechschwarz in die RWY eingebrannt und setzen Taktschwerpunkte für das Schleifern von lamentierenden Bratschen. Sie streichen kräftig an unserer Netzhaut und lassen Geruch von angesengtem Gummi aufkommen. Ein realer und von Technik beherrschter Raum wird plötzlich destabilisiert. Das scheinbare Gleichgewicht von Himmel und Erde will im zweiten Anflugwinkel unserer Bildbetrachtung auf die exakt axialperspektivisch eingefangenen Flugbahnen so harmonisch nicht mehr gelingen. Das eingangs in „Way to beyond" schützende Futteral der friedlichen Landschaft gerät in Bewegung und zeigt tiefe Risse. Es sind die Orte, an die zwei Piloten für einmal nicht mehr zurückgekehrt sind.

In der neunteiligen Folge der „Runways" verknüpft Naomi Leshem alle neun Militärflugplätze des Landes Israel. Im Network des realen nationalen Luftraums über Galiläa, der Mittelmeerküste, dem Westjordanland und dem Wüstengebiet des Negev rückt die rezeptive Aktivität des Betrachters auch die realen Gebiete von Gazastreifen, Golanhöhen und Libanon mit ein. Die stillen Bilder berühren eine Welt, die uns im „Wissen von der Welt" hier wohl stärker beschäftigen als anderswo. Die Fotografin aber durchläuft in diesen Aufnahmen andere und sehr persönliche Prozesse. Auf den „touch down zones", wo die Fahrwerke der Kampfjets aufsetzen, ist kein Ort zum Verweilen. Unser Hineinhören in die Fotografien der still gewordenen RWY steigert die Pistenlandschaften in eine neue Erlebnisrealität voll Hochspannung und menschlicher Sehnsucht. Der Verkehr ruht auf allen neun Landebahnen unter der brennenden Mittagssonne. Es sind Momente der Begegnung mit der grossen Abwesenheit.

Es brauchte höhere Zustimmung, um diese Landebahnen in Wiederholung für Momente betreten zu dürfen. Junge Frauen nehmen einzeln Rollen auf den von den Bremsspuren gezeichneten Laufstegen ein. Präzis ausgeführte Bewegungen scheinen diese ambivalente Wirklichkeit zu vermessen, zu verinnerlichen und abzustossen. Die harten Rennbahnen verlieren ihre Stärke, werden fragil, gleichen gar gebrochenen Rückgraten. Raum und Bewegung fügen sich zu einer Art Schauspiel um Leben und Tod. „Memento mori" (Erinnere dich deiner Sterblichkeit) als fotografischer Mahnruf an die Vergänglichkeit meldet sich. Hans Holbein der Jüngere (1497 – 1543) hat den von Lebensfülle, Lebensgenuss, Spiel und auch Geschäftigkeit strahlenden Standesvertretern in der Zeit grosser Pestkatastrophen Knochenmenschen als Begleiter von drei Dutzend Klienten zugeführt. Die Symbolfiguren, die Naomi Leshem auf die schwarz eingestrichenen Laufstege der RWY treten lässt, schaffen eine Umkehrung der Rollen. Grazien gleich tragen die Mädchen neue Signale voll Leben und Sehnsucht in diese Räume zurück. Der Tod aber bleibt als Erfahrung und Erinnerung vor Ort. Die RWY werden in der sehr persönlichen Arbeit der Künstlerin zum grossen fotografischen Emblem von „Vanitas", von Vergänglichkeit. Die Bilder holen sich das Leben, rennen und schreiten gegen den Tod. Sie formen neues Leben.

Der Zyklus kehrt mit „Lizette" abschliessend nochmals ins Gegenteil, in Ausblicke auf die eitle und schnelllebige Erde der postindustriellen Gegenwart. Suburbane Randzonen wuchern ungezügelt im Ballungsraum von

Tel Aviv. Die Dynamik der Retortenstädte schafft neuen Halt. Die 2007 begonnene Sequenz erweitert die Fotografin kontinuierlich mit immer neuen Aufnahmen vom gleichen Balkon eines Hochhauses in präzisen monatlichen Intervallen. Der immer gleiche Ausblick auf eine sich ständig wandelnde Zwischenstadt-Landschaft mit Wohnburgen, Friedhof, Strassen, Wegen, Feldern, Brachland, Ablagerungen und umgepflügten Feldern. Die Fotografin durchbricht damit das Abgeschlossene und Versiegelte von Geschichte und somit auch das in fotografischen Aufnahmen Festgehaltene und Fixierte. Das fortlaufende Einfangen dieser von Dynamik gezeichneten Landschaft öffnet ein grosses meditatives Fenster auf die nie abgeschlossene Vergänglichkeit. „Lizette" ist Sinnbild für Leben von uns allen und zugleich wie ein Blatt der Riesenseerose, das das ganze Gewicht dieser persönlichen Geschichte von „Vanitas" zu tragen vermag. Stille Erhabenheit, so nahe am Leben.

What Coheres

A deep, warming blue colors the aura of the sacred landscape. A motionless fishing boat on the Sea of Galilee in the morning. This prelude, "Way to beyond", opens by introducing the whole spectrum of continuity and stability recounted by divine and poetic inspiration. Heaven, peace, dreams, and longing shine forth as color tones. Ultramarine reaches from the spirituality of the Jordan Rift Valley into the gentle foothills of Galilee. This space of ethereal power makes textual images from the Bible truthful and audible as tales of events and eternity. Hallowed land and fishing waters are the territory Naomi Leshem embeds us in, a protective covering that is both sensory and metaphorical. The photographer receives us in a controlled, contemplative silence. Why she chose this ideal landscape as the starting point of this four-part cycle remains a secret at first.

"Phantom" breaks with the landscape's blue silence and brings catastrophe into the world. With all the photographic and cinematic means at their disposal, these video images connect reality to death. Death itself now plays the lead, a counterweight to life. Trails of wreckage on the bottom of the Sea of Galilee are the way stations of these rebuses. There are no more horizons. The places have dissolved. It was, it is said, the right wingtip that touched the surface of the lake in the blinding sunlight. You turn toward these images even as you turn away from them. Like the focus of the gaze, language begins to blur. Arbitrarily, like collages, the stills from military videos become groups of witnesses, heralds of death. No voices speak here, and death becomes space. The colors are flat and dull as spotlights search in all directions. A robot with a camera inches across the bottom of the lake. It slows down when visibility decreases, then speeds up in unoccupied terrain. Everywhere, it wants to find and recover things. Between churned-up clouds of sediment lies the mute, fragmented wreckage of the fighter. These are not just marks of a chaotic, deadly topography but also, as traces of aviation technology, messengers from the here and now. Here, we witness an archaeology of things falling apart, of destruction, of the cataloging of the fragments of the wreckage, which no longer clarify life at all. Our turn towards all this constantly turns into a turning away from it all. Everything becomes nothing but an argument for death.

The silent, meditative language of the images in "Runways" turns to the other side of the events documented in "Phantom". Light, color, and warmth reach to distant horizons. Heaven and earth have each other and maintain a strong presence. Their paths carefully guided, our gazes are forced to extremes of concentration, leaping across airstrips, intersections, crossings, markings, safety nets. The runways exist in the pull of the gaze into the distance, but at the same time, they do not exist. The good weather conditions are those called for by the Visual Flight Rules, but the deafening, death-bringing jet fighters have been conjured away, as if by an invisible hand. Even the expected patterns of vapor trails in the sky cannot be found anywhere. Purity and silence have settled in. But one's increasing certainty about where these photographs were taken also feeds one's awareness that this is all a grand illusion. With the photographer, we are standing inside the "displaced threshold" where nobody is permitted to be at all. Restlessness, danger, and uncertainty encroach on us, hostile or even threatening. The pitch-black skid marks of roughly landing tires have burned into the runways, metrical accents for the burnish of lamenting violas, making a powerful impression on our retinas and recalling the smell of burnt rubber. A real space dominated by technology is suddenly destabilized. As we take a second angle of approach to this image of flight paths captured with precise axial symmetry, the apparent equilibrium of heaven and earth no longer seems as harmonious. The protective cover of the peaceful landscape at the beginning of "Way to beyond" shifts, exposing deep rifts. These are the places that two pilots once no longer returned to.

Leshem puts all of Israel's nine military landing fields into the nine-part sequence "Runways". In the net of the real national airspace over Galilee, the Mediterranean coast, and the Negev Desert, the observer's reception of the images also brings to mind the real regions of the Gaza Strip, the West Bank, the Golan Heights, and Lebanon. The silent images touch a world that surely captures our attention here more than elsewhere in our "knowledge of the world". In these photographs, though, the photographer runs through other, quite personal processes. The touchdown zones where the landing gear of the fighters comes to earth are nowhere for anyone to be. Our listening into these photographs of the now silent runways lifts the airfield landscapes into a new experiential reality full of high tension and human longing. There is no traffic on any of the nine airstrips in the burning midday sun. These are moments when we come face to face with the enormity of absence.

Permission for the photographer to go on these landing strips had to be granted at the highest levels. Young women play solitary roles on these skid-marked runways. Their precisely executed movements seem to take the measure of this ambivalent reality, both internalizing it and rejecting it at the same time. The hard asphalt strips lose their strength, grow fragile, even begin to resemble broken backbones. Space and motion connect in a kind of life-and-death drama. This photographic exhortation to transience acts as a Memento mori (remember that you are mortal). In the age of the great plagues, Hans Holbein the Younger (1497 – 1543) provided skeletons to accompany three dozen representatives of the elite, people glowing with fulfillment and the enjoyment of life, with both playfulness and bustle. The symbolic figures Leshem puts on the black-lined catwalks of the runways invert such roles. Like the Graces, these young women put new signals full of life and longing back into these spaces, even as death remains present as experience and memory. In the artist's very personal work, the runways become a great photographic emblem of Vanitas, of transience. The images take life in while running and striding toward death. They form new life.

With "Lizette", the cycle finally returns once more to the opposite, to views of the vain, fast-moving world of contemporary postindustrial society. Suburban fringes run rampant in the Tel Aviv metropolitan area. The dynamism of the planned city establishes a new foundation. The sequence was begun in 2007, and the photographer has continually added to it with new photographs taken from the same high-rise at regular monthly intervals. In each photograph is the same view of a steadily changing landscape of urban sprawl, with a housing development, a cemetery, roads, paths, fields, fallow patches, dumps, and plowed-up land. Here, the photographer breaks open what history closed and sealed, and thus also what photographs catch and freeze. The ongoing capturing of this dynamically marked landscape opens a great meditative window on the never closed past. "Lizette" is a symbol of how we all live, and at the same time, it is like a petal of a giant water lily, bearing the entire weight of this personal tale of Vanitas. Silent sublimity, so close to life.

Naomi Leshem

geboren 1963 in Jerusalem, lebt und arbeitet in Tel Aviv, Israel. Seit 1996 Dozentin für Fotografie an verschiedenen Hochschulen Israels, u.a. am Photography College in Kiryat Ono sowie 1998 – 2005 am Israel Museum in Jerusalem. Fotografien in privaten und öffentlichen Sammlungen in Israel, den USA und Europa. Ausstellungen in Israel (Israel Museum Jerusalem, Tel Aviv Museum), New York, Wien und im März 2009 erstmals in der Schweiz.

Ausgewählte Einzelausstellungen

2009 Galerie Sylva Denzler, Zürich, Schweiz; 2001 „touches", Artists House, Jerusalem, Israel; 2000 „touches", Beit Gavriel, Tiberias, Israel; 1998 Bloomfield Science Museum, Jerusalem, Israel; 1997 „blessed for having made me a woman", The Jerusalem Center for the Performing Arts, Jerusalem, Israel; 1997 „From medium to medium", Tova Osman Gallery, Tel Aviv, Israel; 1996 „From medium to medium", Artists House, Jerusalem, Israel

Ausgewählte Gruppenausstellungen

2008 „mirror, mirror", Tova Osman Gallery, Tel Aviv, Israel; 2007 „moods and modes in Israeli photography", Tel Aviv museum of art, Israel; 2007 „Water in art and life" Israel Museum, Jerusalem, Israel; 2007 „Current visions #2", Andrea Meislin Gallery, New York, USA; 2001 „Hands", Israel Museum, Jerusalem, Israel; 1998 Club Kunstsalon Sommerpalais Harrach, Wien, Österreich; 1997 Artists House, Jerusalem, Israel; 1993 „To live in Jerusalem", Israel Museum, Jerusalem

Werke von Naomi Leshem finden sich in folgenden Sammlungen

Israel Museum, Jerusalem Collection, Israel; Tel Aviv Museum of Art Collection, Tel Aviv, Israel; Private collections in Israel, USA, Germany, Switzerland

Michael Guggenheimer

freier Publizist und Fotograf in Zürich, hat seine Kindheit und Jugend in Tel Aviv und Amsterdam verbracht. Studium der Zeitgeschichte und Sozialpsychologie, zunächst Redakteur bei verschiedenen Zeitungen, anschliessend sieben Jahre lang Öffentlichkeitsarbeit für Kulturprojekte in der Ostschweiz, während dreizehn Jahren Leiter der Abteilung Kommunikation und Pressesprecher der Schweizer Kulturstiftung Pro Helvetia. Autor mehrerer Bücher. Zahlreiche Veröffentlichungen in Zeitungen und Zeitschriften. 2007 zusammen mit Katarina Holländer Kurator der Ausstellung „Ein gewisses jüdisches Etwas" anlässlich des Europäischen Tages der jüdischen Kultur in Zürich, in Zusammenarbeit mit Omanut, dem Verein zur Förderung jüdischer Kunst in der Schweiz, dessen stellvertretender Vorsitzender er ist. 2008 Kurator von zwei Ausstellungen im Stadtmuseum München und im Jüdischen Museum Frankfurt.

Peter Röllin

Dr. phil. Kultur- und Kunstwissenschaftler, geboren 1946 in St. Gallen. Lebt und arbeitet in Rapperswil-Jona / Schweiz als Dozent, Publizist, Forscher, Experte und Ausstellungsmacher. Tätigkeitsbereiche sind u.a. Kulturgeschichte und aktuelle Kulturarbeit, Vermittlung von Veränderungsprozessen und Veränderungserfahrungen im Raum, Theorie und Praxis, Architektur und Städtebau; Kulturprojekte und Kunstvermittlung. Zahlreiche Publikationen zu Architektur- und Stadtbaugeschichte. Inhalt und Szenographie Ostschweizer Pavillon „aua extrema" an der Expo.02 in Neuenburg. Ausstellungen u.a. „Stickerei-Zeit" 1989 im Kunstmuseum St. Gallen, „Stadtbahnhof-Bahnhofstadt Bern" in der Universitätsbibliothek Bern, „Peter Heman, 1919 – 2001: Architektur Photographie" im Architekturmuseum Basel. Peter Röllin ist Leiter der IG Halle Rapperswil (Kunsthalle).

Naomi Leshem

was born in Jerusalem in 1963 and lives and works in Tel Aviv, Israel. Since 1996, she has taught photography at several universities in Israel, including the College of Photography in Kiryat Ono and, from 1998 to 2005, the Israel Museum in Jerusalem. Her photographs are in private and public collections in Israel, the United States and Europe and have been exhibited in Israel (Israel Museum Jerusalem, Tel Aviv Museum), New York and Vienna. Her first exhibition in Switzerland is taking place in June 2009.

Selected Solo Exhibitions
2009 Galerie Sylva Denzler, Zürich, Schweiz; 2001 "touches", Artists House, Jerusalem, Israel; 2000 "touches", Beit Gavriel, Tiberias, Israel; 1998 Bloomfield Science Museum, Jerusalem, Israel; 1997 „blessed for having made me a woman", The Jerusalem Center for the Performing Arts, Jerusalem, Israel; 1997 "From medium to medium", Tova Osman Gallery, Tel Aviv, Israel; 1996 "From medium to medium", Artists House, Jerusalem, Israel

Selected Group Exhibitions
2008 "mirror, mirror", Tova Osman Gallery, Tel Aviv, Israel; 2007 "moods and modes in Israeli photography", Tel Aviv museum of art, Israel; 2007 "Water in art and life" Israel Museum, Jerusalem, Israel; 2007 "Current visions #2", Andrea Meislin Gallery, New York, USA; 2001 "Hands", Israel Museum, Jerusalem, Israel; 1998 Club Kunstsalon Sommerpalais Harrach, Vienna, Austria; 1997 Artists House, Jerusalem, Israel; 1993 "To live in Jerusalem", Israel Museum, Jerusalem

Collections
Israel Museum, Jerusalem Collection, Israel; Tel Aviv Museum of Art Collection, Tel Aviv, Israel; Private collections in Israel, USA, Germany, Switzerland

Michael Guggenheimer

A free-lance journalist and photographer in Zurich, Michael Guggenheimer grew up in Tel Aviv and Amsterdam. After studying Contemporary History and Social Psychology, he first became a newspaper editor before working for seven years in public relations for cultural projects in Eastern Switzerland and for thirteen years as press spokesman and head of the Department of Communications at the Swiss Cultural Foundation Pro Helvetia. He has written a number of books and published widely in newspapers and journals. In 2007, he was the co-curator, with Katarina Holländer, of the exhibition "Ein gewisses jüdisches Etwas", a contribution to the European Day of Jewish Culture in Zurich (a collaboration with Omanut, an organization promoting Jewish culture in Switzerland, of which he is the Vice Chair). In 2008, he curated exhibits in Munich's Stadtmuseum and at the Jewish Museum in Frankfurt.

Peter Röllin

Peter Röllin was born in 1946 in St. Gallen. He has a Ph. D. in Cultural Studies and Art History and lives and works in Rapperswil-Jona, Switzerland, as a lecturer, journalist, researcher, art expert, and curator. His specialties include cultural history and contemporary cultural work, along with the processes and experience of spatial transformation, the theory and practice of architecture and urban planning, and cultural projects and art interpretation. His numerous publications focus mostly on the history of architecture and urban planning. At Expo.02 in Neuchatel, he put on the pavillion "aua extrema" for the cantons of Eastern Switzerland. His other exhibitions include "Stickerei-Zeit" at the Art Museum in St. Gallen in 1989, "Stadtbahnhof-Bahnhofstadt Bern" at the University Library in Bern, and the photography of Peter Heman at the Architecture Museum in Basel. He also runs the IG Halle Rapperswil (the Kunsthalle).

© 2009 Benteli Verlags AG, Bern
© Texte bei den Autoren
© Fotografien bei Naomi Leshem

Herausgeber
Michael Guggenheimer, Zürich
Peter Röllin, Rapperswil-Jona

Gestaltung
2xGoldstein, Karlsruhe (D)

Redaktion und Lektorat
Peter Graf, Zürich

Englische Übersetzung
Andrew Shields, Basel

Fotolithographie und Druck
Heer Druck AG, Sulgen

Buchbinder
Eibert AG, Eschenbach

ISBN 978-3-7165-1582-2

BENTELI Verlags AG
Bern – Sulgen – Zürich
www.benteli.ch

© 2009 Benteli Verlags AG, Berne
© Texts by the authors
© Photographs by Naomi Leshem

Edited by
Michael Guggenheimer, Zürich
Peter Röllin, Rapperswil-Jona

Designed by
2xGoldstein, Karlsruhe (D)

Copy-Edited by
Peter Graf, Zürich

Translated from the German by
Andrew Shields, Basel

Photolithography and printing
Heer Druck AG, Sulgen

Bookbinding
Eibert AG, Eschenbach

ISBN 978-3-7165-1582-2

BENTELI Publishers
Berne – Sulgen – Zurich
www.benteli.ch

Dank
Künstlerin, Herausgeber und
Verlag danken folgenden Personen
und Institutionen, die durch
ihre Unterstützung massgeblich
zur Realisation des vorliegenden
Buches beigetragen haben:

Thanks
The artist, the editors and the
publishing house thank following
persons and institutions whose
support contributed significantly
to the realization of this book:

**Dr. Georg und
Josi Guggenheim-Stiftung**

Georges und Jenny Bloch-Stiftung

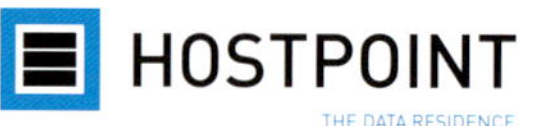